Living and Growing in Later Years

Living and Growing in Later Years.

LLOYD H. AHLEM

Covenant Benevolent Institutions, Inc.
5145 North California Avenue
Chicago, Illinois 60625

ISBN 0-9626063-1-6

Design and layout: David Westerfield
Production: Covenant Publications

TABLE OF CONTENTS

FOREWORD

Fred and I had just finished a hotly contested golf game and Fred had won. He was sweaty but grinning—having subdued me, twenty years his junior. He was a vigorous person, ruddy but in great physical shape for a man in his mid-seventies. "I don't understand it," he blurted. "I feel as good as I did 30 years ago; my game is better than ever, I have no health problems and I've been retired almost ten years. Where are all the problems I've been hearing about? Do you suppose all the stuff I read in the papers about people my age is just baloney? They seem to be aching, groaning, going deaf, yet living longer, getting diseases I never heard of, and undergoing all kinds of medical procedures we never dreamed about when I was a kid. I don't know what to expect or what to believe about getting old. Maybe it won't happen to me!" "It probably will, Fred," I replied, "but there is plenty of both myth and truth that needs to be sorted out. Be thankful you are doing so well and keep doing it!" Fred is not unusual. We need to dispel some myths and confirm some facts about aging. Most people enter their later years with both misinformation and truth in their heads. In later years, seniors are surprised again and again by what normally transpires. The purpose of this book is to help clear up some of the questions we all face in the aging process.

For the past decade I have been privileged to serve as director of Covenant Village, a retirement center in Turlock, California. After seventeen years in higher education and eight in public school psychology and private practice, my career with youth had taken an abrupt turn. Though surprises and discoveries were frequent, work with older people has been most gratifying. Observing aging first-hand, I had the opportunity to sort out my own sack of garbled ideas about getting old and think through the adjustments older people must make. This volume is developed with those observations in mind. Each chapter deals with an important issue facing older adults. Questions for discussion follow so that the volume may serve as a study guide for seniors, their adult children, or groups interested in older people. The text is also a formalization of seminars presented throughout North America.

The retirement center I served is a training site for interns, students who earn master's degrees in public administration, gerontology, or long-term care. Some of these interns completed research projects that helped to sharpen my insights and keep my academic instincts alive. They also assisted me in completing a major study of the quality of life in nine Covenant Retirement Communities that further confirmed and dispelled many of my ideas about aging. My special thanks to my staff: Dorothy, Ken, Aila, Elaine, Dick, John, Gladys, Phil, Sue, Rudy, a number of interns, and an ever-changing group of 90 service personnel. Thanks also to great top corporate leadership of Covenant Retirement Communities under Nils G. Axelson and Paul V. Peterson, as well as the residents who are a treasure of blessing and grace. Many have become great friends and models for Christian life in a community of older people.

Lloyd H. Ahlem
Covenant Village of Turlock
Turlock, California 1992

ONE

Common Myths of Aging

Myth #1: Older people are all one type. A youngster came bounding into the lobby of our retirement center once and bustled up to the receptionist. "I came to see my grandma's sister," he announced. "Do you know where I can find her?"

"What is her name and what does she look like?" responded the receptionist. "She's about five feet two, has gray hair, wears glasses, and her name is either Anderson or Carlson."

"That describes more than half of the ladies who live here," replied the receptionist. "I guess we'll have to hunt a bit."

The child's description is a part of the stereotype we often assign to older people—one I have fallen victim to myself. When I was young, I mistakenly had the notion that all people over 65 were old, looked alike, thought alike, communicated alike, and misunderstood everybody who was 20 or more years younger. Now that I am joining their ranks I am quickly changing my view. I still wonder why I wake up in the morning feeling young, only to look in the mirror and see my father. But I have learned that older people are unique and individual.

In the retirement homes where I worked, the age range is more than 40 years. That's as long as the working life of most adults! When I began employment, the youngest member of our community was 58 and quite ill. The oldest was 98 and quite well. In fact, the latter survived several years after the former had passed away. Although they lived in the same center, they had little in common: different ages, different interests and activities, and different physical problems. So the myth of homogeneity—the idea that one description fits all—was shattered promptly.

A good friend of mine was widowed at 72. He took his loss well, though painfully, and recovered to enjoy life again. Soon he found a widowed lady whose company he enjoyed and pursued ardently. Watching them in their courtship was like observing a teenage romance. They had more in common emotionally with high school young people than with their own age mates. They grinned, blushed, held hands, said sweet nothings to each other, and acted as if the whole world was an idyllic dream designed for their pleasure. Both had great marriages previously, a fact that predicted their new marriage would go well, too. Both had grown children, were free of financial worries, and had entered into their vocations with genuine zest. Who were their peers? Newlyweds, not old-timers in rocking chairs.

Or I think of a gentleman who had spent his life in China as a missionary. He had survived the Boxer Rebellion, the Japanese invasion of China, and repatriation to the U.S. He was still enthusiastic about life and his mission in it. On the seventieth anniversary of his graduation from North Park College, he was awarded an honorary doctoral degree. His son, who had become chief of the Asian Desk in the U.S. State Department, was on hand to witness the ceremonies. It was a happy moment for us all. I later called on the man to see how he was getting along. I could tell that I was an intruder that day but he invited me in, visited a bit, and then asked me to find my way out. He was working on a commentary on the book of Isaiah and wanted to finish it promptly. "Call again," he cheerily offered, "when I'm not so busy." The myth that older people have lost their intellectual acuity and creativity was shattered to bits by watching him work and think out loud. At least in that regard he had more in common with graduate students than his age mates.

I also recall a lady who never had the opportunity for much schooling. She and her husband had lost their small business during the Great Depression and never fully recovered. But in her advanced years a latent aptitude came quickly to life. She always had a flair for decorating, and her home was a delight to see—especially at Christmas. At age 80 she began to paint, under the tutelage of a teacher who recognized her possibilities. Within a year's time she had developed some fine technique to amplify her native talent. Appreciative buyers bought most of her work. That created a problem, of course. Her Social Security payments were reduced because of her rising income. But so what? A new lift in life had come to her. She was not creatively dead and nowhere near decline, even though her remaining years were clearly limited. As regarded her art, she had more in common with young art majors than with her friends down the hall.

Or consider the 94 year old who learned to trade in the stock market and tripled his net worth in his last six years. Or the couple that regained such good health in a retirement center that they left, went into missions, and worked as volunteers. They outlived their normal life expectancies by a good number of years. The myth that older people are a homogeneous population in regard to any aspect of life is a myth that needs scrapping.

Myth #2: Older people live in loneliness and isolation. While I know of some who suffer this way, it is because they have chosen remote lifestyles. When age advances, this detachedness traps them and does not serve their needs. When illness comes, they have no one to call. If they need help to keep house or want to take a trip, they cannot do so because they are so withdrawn. But their problem is not a matter of age as much as it is of earlier life choices. Those who have established long-term relationships through churches and friendship groups don't have nearly so much difficulty.

I remember trying to get an appointment with an older friend who had retired to Florida. I was to be in his area a short time and wanted to see him regarding a business matter. But his calendar was so full of dinner parties, church meetings, visiting shut-ins, helping the local college, and playing golf, that he had no time for me. The only way to find him was to plan well in advance. Then he heartily welcomed me and we had wonderful visits. He was a walking encyclopedia on the restaurants of southwest Florida, so our visits were usually jolly and caloric. He died at 90, happy and overweight!

His life was not too different from many like him. With the freedom that retirement brings, he moved into more activities than ever before. And he loved it thoroughly! The myth of loneliness and isolation won't stand up to such evidence. The few who have made poor choices and now suffer should not be forgotten. Severe loneliness is a great tragedy but it can readily be averted. But the solution must be found well ahead of the appearance of the problem.

Myth #3: Older persons suffer much sensory loss, such as in sight and hearing. The key word is "much." It is true that most older people wear glasses and some wear hearing aids, but the idea that seniors are generally deaf and can't see where they are going is pure balderdash. In seminars I have conducted on problems of aging, 98 percent of the attendees are wearing glasses. Those that don't often have them in their pockets or are wearing contact lenses. About 30 percent have hearing aids but neither of these problems are true impairments. Life is seldom limited, for hearing aids and glasses enhance the sensory abilities that remain.

Recent advances in cataract surgery, lens implantation, medication for glaucoma, miniaturization of hearing devices, stapes surgery, and the like have given older people wonderful protection from loss of regular contact with the world and their friends. The notion that most have serious problems, therefore, is still a myth.

Myth #4: With age comes rigidity of attitude. My basis for believing this myth is false is a comparison with younger people. I spent a number of years teaching undergraduate courses in psychology, most of it in state colleges. In large part, that teaching was done in the passionate years of campus upheaval—when politics and values were being debated, trashed, or remodeled. I discovered that the most rigid attitudes were held by college freshmen and sophomores. They were being exposed to a world of conflicting ideas for the first time, with very little experience or knowledge against which to test them. Many gave up home-built values during these heated times, but often only to change from one rigid position to another. I remember a radical conservative who become a radical liberal in one afternoon! His move was revolutionary but showed no improvement in thinking; it was merely a flip-flop of positions.

In contrast, I have found that most seniors, having lived through a couple of wars, and having survived both depression and boom time, have a good sense of perspective on world affairs. Their education may have been informal, but exposure to world events and access to information through the media in their time has been the greatest in history. Their reasoned conclusions about matters may be quite firm, but that is not the same as being rigid in thought. They have seen the shades of gray in complex issues and have had to reconcile conflicting ideas. Many ideas believed to be new and revolutionary for the young are old stuff for senior citizens. Ideas that appear to be siren songs for kids cause older people to say, "Here we go again!"

Furthermore, ideas held by seniors were more likely to have been tested in a better spiritual-moral environment. In Malcolm Muggeridge's resignation as rector of the University of Edinburgh, " . . . he complained that the students on whom society lavished its resources in the expectation that they would spearhead progress, producing great works of art, perception, and understanding, were degrading themselves with the resort to any old slobbering debauchee anywhere in the world at any time—Dope and Bed . . . . So he urged students to turn from the faddish art and literature of the university world . . .as from bad dreams of a materialistic world."[1] Thankfully, a lot of youngsters are much better than that, but Muggeridge makes his point.

The advance of secular materialism has deprived the young of the great standards for sensitive thought. Genuine spiritual consensus in universities and most of society has been disintegrating seriously. Clear thinking is more difficult and less valid when timeless truths are ignored or abandoned as checks on present values. Seniors, therefore—with a better spiritual heritage diffuse in their culture and with the sobering experiences of age—are often better and more sensitive thinkers.

Myth #5: Older people are too tired to fight. Some presume that seniors have lost their zip and let conflict roll past them without getting involved. While this may be partly true, it is more likely that older people are picking their ground and not wasting energy on matters of little importance. Having selected an issue to argue they persist as long and as ardently as necessary to make their point. Just as they have refined their thinking and have flexibility in their views, so they have refined their strategies and reasoned their positions. When they fight, they fight knowingly and efficiently. They will not die on every hill that someone needs to defend—only on what they consider the important ones, and then with well-honed skill.

One of the benefits of age is that you can choose your time, your ground, and your weapons. Your work schedule is likely reduced so you can pick your spots and call your shots. When your opponent is preoccupied and stressed about other matters, you can catch him or her at a disadvantage. Furthermore, there are enough of you that you can mount a mighty campaign if you choose to battle in the larger political arena where numbers count. I have seen seniors wear away the resistance of city officials just by their kindly presence, getting them to solve problems that would otherwise be ignored. Just observe the clout of AARP as its members heap thousands of letters on legislators' desks. Seniors fight well, but not on every battlefield.

Myth #6: Older people want to disengage from active living. Disengagement theory has been fairly strong, even in good universities, until recent years. Scholars presumed that both the energy and interest of seniors had waned and that disinterest was the mode of mental life. What we now find, however, is that some interests are more selectively pursued and lesser ones pushed aside. Just as oldsters fight more efficiently and selectively, interests also become focused. Seniors select what interests them from lesser options.

Many younger people perceive time as the enemy of the old. They see years adding up and believe that shortening life means lessening of opportunity. But I find that time is more likely the ally of the aged. With the benefits of retirement programs and pensions and the freedom from distractions and obligations of younger years, seniors concentrate on interests much more efficiently than at any time in the past.

I think of a friend who served as a college dean for many years. He was skilled and able, but the trivia and detail in his work pushed him away from his greatest gift—writing reflective biographies. His irritation mounted until he took early retirement and concentrated on his greatest interest. In a few years he wrote more than he had in three-and-one-half decades of managing academic machinery. Time would not pass quickly enough in his administrative career; now time stretched before him uncluttered and seldom interrupted. He was far more satisfied and unfettered than ever. Time had become his friend, whereas previously it was an enemy to be subdued until he could get on with his dreams.

Myth #7: Old people are more depressed than younger people. It is true that cases can be found where depression is seriously affecting an older person. But most often that is due to a particular clinical problem such as glandular malfunctioning, lack of blood supply to the brain, or some genetic tendency toward depression. From my reading I conclude that there are two ages when depression is most frequent. The first is in the late teens and early twenties. Youngsters are getting out of school, facing uncertainties of employment, economics, military service, and entering into marriage and family responsibilities—all without self-understanding and fully comprehending their abilities. They are untested people in a testy world. Self-doubt runs high. If one's background has been emotionally shaky, the ups and downs just ahead can be scary. Given such doubt and uncertainty, depression is a frequent result.

Interestingly, the second age of depression is normally in the early forties. Maybe these folks are depressed because some are parents of the twenty year olds! By 40 you have had your education or you have not; you have started child rearing or you have not; you have established yourself in a career pattern or you have not; your belief system is in place—for better or worse—and your remaining years are less than the years you have lived. You also likely believe the myth just spoken about—that time is your enemy, not your ally. Age 40 becomes the time to come to terms with life.

Reflective questioning occupies your quiet moments. Should you have made different choices? Should you make a career change and start over? Should you shed your mate and take a fling? Should you try to acquire the things you have missed thus far? Contemplating your uncertainty, you sit in your easy chair, watch the evening array of disasters on TV, and grouse. You are depressed.

But by the time you are 70 you are long removed from most of this self-doubt and can focus your energy again. Hopefully you have settled most issues, come to terms with your creator, and don't have a lot of uncertainties gnawing at you. Age 40 provides choice opportunities that can set you up for happy times. Yet, or if ignored or misused, it can leave questions that will bother you for years. Age may dull the barbs of unsettled questions, but some will remain. As for death, I find few older people worried very much about it—even those not well-prepared spiritually. Age tends to dull the spiritual question, and while this avoids some stress, it is also a lost opportunity that is hard to retrieve.

Myth #8: Most older people are physically incapacitated in some way. That is straight-out false. The fact is that most organs of your body will work quite well up to the point of death. Most people are 95 percent well when they die. Its that other miserable five percent that is the problem. Like an automobile when one critical part goes bad, the body cannot function without a heart, brain, or liver. So at some point all our machinery stops.

Nevertheless, people fear being confined to a wheel chair or suffering the loss of their mind or senses. Some do suffer handicaps, but most remain quite well most of their days. Only five to ten percent spend time in a nursing home. Most live in their own homes until death. There may be some critical final illness, but these are usually brief rather than extended. So much media attention has been given to problems of the few aged people who are institutionalized that fears of handicap are needlessly exaggerated.

A young friend recently visited a nursing home and afterward came directly to my office, sick to his stomach. "I just saw three people in wheel chairs being fed by nurses," he blurted. "They had no more sense of what was happening to them than the man in the moon. Deliver me from a fate like that! If I get so bad I don't know what's happening to me, just knock me in the head!" We talked awhile, until he got his feelings under control. Then I told him my belief that loss of awareness is often a gift. This thought startles those unacquainted with incapacity, but such loss may well be a blessing. If the suffering one was truly aware of his or her condition life might be intolerable. The greatest difficulty is for loved ones who remember better days and see only the impairments. If they abandon them as they may be tempted to do, they create guilt for themselves. It's far better to accept the handicap, be thankful for former days, and recall that impairments mask the pain.

Most of these myths arise because of fear or lack of understanding. Furthermore, fear and misunderstanding prey upon each other. I know retirees who live within a few yards of a nursing facility but never visit patients. They don't want to be reminded of the possibility that they might one day be there. One such lady abandoned her best friend this way. Her friend had a stroke that immobilized her. But her mental capacities were unaffected and she was pleasant to visit. Yet the friend never came. It was a needless loss. If the courage to visit had been mustered a time or two, understanding would have quickly erased the fear and a happy friendship would have been maintained.

The old and ill need love and care just as always. Those with lessened capacity have not had their emotional needs diminished. Nursing home patients who are only minimally aware of their surroundings need the love of friends and family as much as ever. They may no longer be able to express their need, but the need exists nonetheless. I admire caregivers who stay with the old and disabled when friends and relatives have stopped filling their needs. If you are believing any of the myths mentioned, there is something you can do about your problem. Become aware, seek the truth, face your fears, and meet some needs.

Jim was widowed at 70 and suffered his loss terribly. Lonely, with dreams collapsed, he struggled to regain his morale and hope. But Jim had always wanted to learn to fly and thought this might be the time to try. He enrolled in ground school, passing his tests in just a couple of weeks. Shortly he began flight instruction and in a couple more weeks he was ready to solo. "Go get your medical clearance," his teacher ordered. "You're as ready as your going to get." Jim headed off to see a doctor who could give him clearance and took the usual exam. "You are fit as a fiddle!" the doctor pronounced. "Great!" responded Jim, "Now just sign my flight clearance." "Hey Jim, you're 70 years old; you shouldn't be flying; I can't sign that thing," replied the physician. Disappointed, Jim walked away, but shortly decided to try another doctor. Again the appropriate exam was given and Jim was pronounced in excellent health. "Thanks, doctor," responded Jim. "Now just sign my clearance so I can fly." "Jim, you're 70 years old; you've got no business flying! I can't sign that paper!" Once again, Jim turned away disappointedly. He went back to his flight instructor and told him the bad news. "Jim, I know a doctor who understands these things and he won't turn you down because of age. And he's well-enough regarded that nobody will overrule him, either. Give him a call," suggested the instructor. Once again Jim trudged off to see a physician who found him to be in great condition. That doctor happily signed Jim's flight clearance. "When are you going out to solo?" the doctor inquired. "I want to be there when you take your first flight!" "Are you kidding?" Jim retorted. "I'm 70 years old; nobody's going to get me to fly at my age!" So Jim believed the myth and became a victim of his self-imposed limitation, an experience not uncommon for older people.

Before discussing several truths about aging, let's note a survey that illustrates the point we have been making. In a Lou Harris poll the needs of the elderly were studied.[2] Over 4,000 respondents were asked how they viewed the needs of older people. Approximately half of those questioned were over 65 and half were under 65.

How the Elderly Are Viewed by Others and Themselves*

How Those 18-64 View the Elderly	The Issue	How the Over 65 View Themselves
16	Not Enough Clothing	3
28	Not Enough Friends	5
50	Elderly Are Afraid of Crime	23
54	Elderly Don't Feel Needed	7
60	Elderly Faced with Loneliness	12
29	Elderly Are Bright and Alert	68
35	Elderly Get Things Done	55
21	Elderly Open-minded, Adaptable	63
82	Elderly Friendly and Warm	72

**all numbers represent percentages*

The differences between the two groups illustrate the point that myths prevail. Harris's conclusion is: "The portrait of mature citizens drawn by those who have not reached maturity is that of unalert, physically inert, narrowminded, ineffective, sexually finished old people rotting away in poor health, without proper medical care and without enough money to live on. What is more the truth is that older people are alert, moderately active, sexually able, socially inclined with broad interests, feeling needed by family and friends, with intellectual and creative abilities intact.

Harris further suggests that older people have been brain-washed by these stereotypes so that they believe them about themselves and may live as if the stereotypes were true. It is apparent that whatever is done for older persons must be done to educate the younger set as well. The misperceptions of both older and younger people may have become cherished ignorance and a significant obstacle to learning about later years.

References

1. Muggeridge, Malcolm, The End of Christendom, (Grand Rapids, Michigan: 1980), p. xii. From the introduction by John S. North.
2. As reported in the AARP News Bulletin, Vol. XV, No. 10, November, 1974.

Questions for Discussion

1. Which of the myths have you been most inclined to believe in your recent past? Why? Which myths have you rejected most easily? Why?
2. Why do you think such myths arise? What sources of information give rise to common myths?
3. Are there other beliefs about aging you now hold that might be suspect? What leads you to believe they may be untrue?
4. Have you ever resisted believing a truth because of a long-believed myth? What feelings did you discover when this conflict occurred?
5. Do you know older people who believe such myths about themselves? Do they resist truths that might be of help to them? How do they react in the face of changing belief?
6. What can you do in your church and community to reduce beliefs in these myths?

TWO

Truths of Aging

There are more older people in our society, both in number and proportion, than at any time in history.[1] Thirty-two million people will be over 65 in America in the year 2000. People over 65 now outnumber teenagers in our country. This affects every political and social agenda in America. Older adults vote; teenagers don't. Guess whose needs will get attention! With the graying of the populations in North America, consider the following:

1) Three-generation families are the rule, not the exception. Most of us knew our grandparents. Now we're getting to know great-grandparents as well. At age 80 you have a 75 percent chance of being a four-generation family. My granddaughter was the first in our family to know her great grandmothers well, visiting them in the nursing home where they lived. "Great-grandmother Jensen," she chortled, "as soon as you are well I will take you swimming!" The great grandmother had a tremendous laugh!

We once thought our grandparents had many children. Now, with multiple generations, mobility, divorce, and remarriage, our children have many parents. Extended families are common, but are they closely knit enough to nourish healthy offspring with tender care? We often speak of the sandwich generation, middle-aged folks parenting their children as well as their parents. Pressures can be smothering if you are in the sandwich. Imagine parenting your children *plus* both parents and grandparents! This is rare, but it is possible. A 50-year-old woman I knew had a 68-year-old mother and an 88-year-old grandmother as well as teenage children. All three adult women were single and on welfare. The two oldest required help, from buttons to bathroom to bedtime. The fifty year old became program director for four generations. No wonder she was tired! Her teenagers were normally testy, trying to become somebody, while the older ones were becoming more dependent. While few people will face this problem, it is one of the mixed blessings of living longer.

2) People over 65 have twice as many doctor's visits, use 39 percent of hospital time (though they comprise 12 percent of the population), and stay twice as long during each stay. About ten million admissions occur each year. With changing government regulations and reimbursement dollars, hospitals hardly know how to plan. Physicians are becoming gerontologists whether they want to be or not.

Hospital visits are shortening as Medicare limits lengthy stays, and much more outpatient service is rendered. One retiree was 94 years old when he needed hernia surgery. He was told that Medicare would only pay for one night's stay so he walked home the day after surgery. Fortunately his son took him in until he had recovered a little more. How many 90 year olds would have been able to accommodate Medicare's demand?

As bacterial diseases are conquered, older people are exposed more to viral and nervous system diseases. These are more difficult to cure, and often require specialized care. So we live longer and die more expensively! Many older people who have lived a long time without health insurance wonder if they should have it now. I know 90 year olds who got their first health insurance when they were in their seventies, and resent having to pay for it. But the consequences of not being insured are devastating—particularly in extended-care facilities where neither Medicare nor health-care insurance provides coverage.

3) Many high stress events normally occur during advanced years: death, costly illnesses, loss of purchasing power on fixed incomes, loss of a spouse, and changes in self-image associated with retirement status. We will speak more of these later when we discuss the transitions in aging these events set up. But the fact is that some of life's most stressful normal experiences occur during a short number of our later years. Special strategies may be needed.

We know, for example, that a delicate balance exists between the endocrine and nervous systems. In advanced years these systems are less efficient, functioning quite differently from people in their twenties. So the balance between systems changes as well. The result can be a very different feeling about oneself. For example, reduced functioning of the thyroid may be related to depressed feelings.

Depression can lead one to believe he or she has done something wrong or is of little value to anyone. The solution is not spiritual or emotional, but most likely some thyroid medication taken under a doctor's supervision. Then the psychological side-effects can be worked out. Similarly, the liver does not work nearly as efficiently as it once did. If an older person is accustomed to a Martini or two before supper, he or she may now appear to be an inebriate. Friends may think the individual has hit the bottle to cloud realities of aging. Moralizing from friends seldom helps; good medical counsel can alleviate the problem much more readily. Regular medical surveillance is a must. Irregular surveillance and ignorance lead to over- or under-medication, and tangle up emotional life.

The stressful event that surprised me most as to its severity is the experience of being forced to change living quarters. Whether removed from a long-time personal residence or transferred to a nursing home, the jolt can be traumatic, even more severe than losing a spouse. According to Holmes and Rahe, becoming a widow is clearly the toughest normal adjustment one has to make.[2] However, as we interviewed retirees, we discovered that most of them anticipated losing a spouse and did a lot of grieving and planning ahead of time, often openly with their mates. They knew life would be much different after the loss, but took time to get ready for the changes. Yet a forced change in living quarters usually comes as a surprise. Sometimes it's anticipated, but most people do not adjust ahead of time. In our retirement centers we prepare people to avoid as much surprise as possible when a move must be made. Some do not welcome a conversation suggesting they should ready themselves for this awful disruption. But talking about it is helpful. A little anger ahead of time relieves the stress of moving later and aids eventual adjustment. Those who are allowed to worry productively make better moves.

4) In advanced years, the basis for self-image changes. We must shift from external to internal sources to tell us we are worthy people. But when the internal sources are lacking, self-image takes a licking. It is not uncommon for older people to feel useless and a bother to others. If they have built self-concepts from their achievements rather than from their intrinsic spiritual values, they are especially vulnerable.[3]

Ann D. was a well-recognized illustrator for a large metropolitan newspaper. Her work was solicited until she was in her later seventies. But then the drawings became simplistic and crude. Minor strokes were robbing her of her creativity. For several years thereafter she maintained her studio and struggled to draw but was ignored by the publishers. In her anxiety, she produced a greater volume of illustrations than ever, only to stuff them—soaked with tears—into the refuse bins. Her self-picture had been destroyed. Healthy self-image for most people is built on several bases.[4] If these bases are lacking, personality problems usually result. These bases are:

a) Success in a field to which one aspires. When we are successful in something we want to do, we feel good about ourselves. If we are marginally successful or a failure, we are unhappy and feel bad about ourselves. We lack confidence and become dreary people to live with. If we succeed in a field we are not particularly interested in, our feelings are not much affected. Or if we fail in something that is unimportant to us, we are not greatly bothered. But when we fail in that to which we are highly committed, we are miserable. People long overmatched by their ambitions reach older years with unfortunate personality wrinkles. As years advance it is important to adjust goals to keep them within reach. Many possibilities for achievement, however, are removed by retirement, especially for men. If they have little meaningful activity to engage them or have no sense of internal, intrinsic value, retirement can be discouraging.

b) A sense of power or control over our lives. If we feel we can make things happen that enhance us we have a great deal of confidence. Conversely, if we feel we are constantly a victim of circumstances, our morale will be low. Children reared with all sense of power residing in their parents seldom grow up confidently. Similarly, when seniors lose power over decisions in their lives, morale suffers. Patients in nursing facilities do better when they can exercise as much control as possible over their lives, even if they make some mistakes that upset the care givers.

c) Conformity to one's moral standards. Misery and bad self-image are the company of people who feel guilty about their behavior. Strangely, there are people who have high ethical behavior who feel terrible about themselves. Their problem is they have no hope of reaching the standards they have set for themselves. No wonder they are discouraged! Likewise, there are people whose behavior is reprehensible to us, who don't feel much guilt. Living in conformity to very low standards they sense that little is wrong. If these standards are so low as to be detrimental to society, such people are regarded as sociopathic. They have never learned healthy guilt and need a good shot of it.

False guilt resulting from excessively high standards can be as damaging as guilt generated from truly immoral activity. Occasionally we find elderly people who are morally "squeaky clean" and miserable in their guilt. They need forgiveness more for falsely high expectations than for their behavior. They may be living with sins no gracious God can remember, simply because they have never learned to forgive themselves. In contrast, however, one of the most beautiful experiences of aging is seen in life nobly lived, fully forgiven, genuinely optimistic, and entirely hopeful. Such is the life lived solely by the grace of God.

Most unfortunate is the person who is old and morally insensitive. He or she has neither learned decent standards nor been compelled to live by any. One can be ugly and aged; and such character is generated out of this background. With moral sense dulled, and self-interests focused on selfish needs, life is degraded and grubby.

d) Physical appearance and self-image. When we are young we bestow much approval on the virile and good looking. We are devoted to the cult of the beautiful. The best rewards go to those who are photogenic. Kids with the best physiognomy and least pimples get the most dates and adulation. A recent issue of a magazine aimed for older readers displayed improbably good-looking seniors on its cover. Even their bathing suit figures belied their ages. Strange that such irreality should be paraded before us when we know the truth! I am sure that beauticians suffer most from those who expect to have their youthful images restored.

If our self-worth is based entirely upon these four qualities, we are going to have trouble with ourselves in advanced years. Age removes most of those achievements from us. We will tire of wearing a cheery mask of success when we feel awful inside. A colleague of mine often said, "You become what you are when you are old. The masks come off and you lack the means to put them back on." Most will feel economic power wane though some will still keep a bit of economic clout—though it won't buy back many of your losses. Everyone will fail to look like a campus homecoming king or queen.

In contrast, the most beautiful people I know are undefensive, warm to everyone, caring for the needs of others, unapologetic about quirks of aging minds, never trying to control others, and always asking what more they can do for you. The indispensable basis for healthy self-image in later years is gratefulness and hope—both abundantly supplied by faith in Christ and by having lived a life devoted to sharing his love. Their vision of eternity helps dismiss the troubles of life as easily as possible.

5) In advanced years we find out who the God is we've chosen to serve. Most people have a creedal statement about the nature of the God they worship, but how they allow that God to function in their beings may be another matter. People who don't call themselves religious have also chosen a god. It may lack verbal formulation, or only be a faith that there is order in the universe. But some god is there, nevertheless. Man is incurably worshipful. In the words of Dorothy Thompson, "The instinct to worship is hardly less strong than the instinct to eat." [5] There is no person without a center of existence which serves as his or her god and object of worship.

William Jennings Bryan affirmed the matter clearly: "Man is a religious being; the heart instinctively seeks for a God whether he worships on the banks of the Ganges, prays with his face upturned to the sun, kneels towards Mecca or, regarding all space as a temple, communes with the Heavenly Father according to the Christian creed; man is essentially devout." [6] And from Thomas Carlyle: "The man who does not habitually worship is but a pair of spectacles behind which there are no eyes." [7] In old age we discover whether our chosen god was true or false, functional or dysfunctional, meaningful or banal, redemptive or damning. We learn fully whether our god has been a cosmic servant to do our bidding or whether we have served a living God with purposes greater than ourselves.

Keith Miller, in *Hunger for Healing*, speaks of firing old gods and embracing a new God, one that bears the likeness of Jesus.[8] Old age gives us a brief opportunity to unload the unholy gods we have chosen to serve us and seek our redemption in the Savior of Holy Scripture. Taking such a step will surely feel perilous! Alfred North Whitehead, mathematician and president of Harvard University describes it thus: "The worship of God is not a rule of safety—it is an adventure of the spirit, a flight after the unattainable."[9] Selfish control begins to slip away and we want to hang on. The deeply ingrained habit of looking out for Number One dies hard. Yet Matthew 10:39 remains true: "He who loses his life for my sake will find it." Sam Shoemaker, well known Episcopal preacher, suggested that if exercising faith in Christ is a fearsome problem, try a thirty-day prayer experiment. Don't pay any attention to whether you can believe adequately; just pray that God will meet you at the point of your need and see what happens to you. That act of faith will lead you to the content of faith and you will be able to surrender to God who loves you and wants to see you through.

The effects of spiritual life are cumulative. If you have worshiped a god only designed to serve you, that god leaves you painfully short. All your views of yourself and your relationships will be distorted by the "me first" attitude of such worship. Normal life requires continual cleansing to keep guilt under control and self-justification from taking us over. But worshiping the God of the Bible who can remove sins "as far as the east is from the west" will generate clear self-perception and great joy, even in declining years.

A favorite text of mine is in 1 Corinthians 2:9: "For eye has not seen nor ear heard nor has there entered into the mind of man the things that God has prepared for them that love him." Whether you sing or sulk your way into eternity will depend directly upon the God you have chosen to redeem you. Having settled upon our beliefs, the truth of our systems or the lack of it comes home to roost. I recall a difficult conversation with a lady who had followed a cult most of her life. She had been a rebel against the orthodoxy of her parents and had made many selfish choices in younger days. In her eighties peace still eluded her as she faced death from a serious stroke. But she cherished her rebellion and could not make sense of her cultic belief either. She spent her last days screaming at friends who gave her Christian counsel, drawing cult leaders to her bedside for assurance they could not furnish. She died in spiritual chaos—the result of commitment to a faith system that could not console or forgive her self-centered life.

C.S. Lewis suggests that to everyone who has never said to the heavenly Father, "Thy will be done;" the Father will respond similarly, "Then *thy* will be done."[10] Thus the individual gets to live forever with the promises of the god he or she has chosen to serve. All the false gods will be unable to deliver redemption and eternal separation will result. God never invades the sovereignty of human will. He only asks gently for its surrender. Then he enters and remakes us in his image and redeems every aspect of our being. Old fears and guilt dissolve. He exceeds our highest estimate of his grace in our behalf. Peace is ours; eternity invites us and we eagerly enter.

6) Children of older people are peers to their parents, neither

parents or dependents. Earlier we mentioned the sandwich generation—middle aged adults parenting their kids as well as their parents. This is increasingly common, but in most instances older people don't need parenting and can manage their own affairs until shortly before death.

My father died at age 66, long before I was ready to part with him. My grief was great and I was angry at his passing because we were becoming friends as peers rather than as father and son. We enjoyed long talks about our histories as well as my future. His insight was unique because he knew me so well. During his last days I learned that I was going to be offered a college presidency two thousand miles away. I was having a wretched time deciding whether or not to uproot my family and thrust such an adventure upon them. As we talked I became keenly aware he was advising me as a fellow, not as a father. He was totally willing to let the decision be mine with the counsel of God. Then he said, "I think you should forget the whole thing," not avoiding telling me his view about the matter. I did not follow his counsel, but I did not have the slightest feeling I should give him any reasons why. He truly set me free. Surely this is how a relationship should be.

In contrast, I know older parents who have never loosened the reins on their children. Later, when the parents become dependent, the relationship is almost unmanageable. The seniors give incompetent or unrealistic orders to mature children who resent being bossed and feel guilty for not obeying. But if they obeyed they would also feel guilty for implementing bad advice—a no-win situation for both parents and children. Fortunately this is the exception more than the rule and most parents set children free to become peers—neither the parents nor the dependents of their sons and daughters.

7) The needs of the old are a changing political issue. If you were born at the creation of America, your life expectancy was about 35 years. Infant deaths plagued families and infectious diseases claimed many more during growing years. A few grew to maturity and old age, but the total number of people over 65 was very small. Social Security was unknown, retirement communities were unnecessary, and heroic life-saving measures that extend life were nearly nonexistent.

But life expectancy has doubled—in just over 200 years! In 1988 the number of Americans over 65 exceeded the number of teenagers. By the year 2000, almost 35 million of us will be over 65. By the year

2050, over 65 million have reached that age. The ramifications of these facts are endless for medicine, politics, economics, housing, employment, and changing family structures. Consider the situation in California.[11] Three streams of immigrants have arrived. Hispanics from Central America and Mexico find our borders a minor obstacle. Many cities are populated by a majority whose native tongue is Spanish. Virtually every school system teaches English as a second language to substantial numbers of children. The second group comes from the rest of the U.S. They moved in large numbers during and after World War II and continue to arrive, seeking employment in high tech industry and sunbelt life styles. The third group has come from the orient: Koreans, Filipinos, Vietnamese, Thais, and a variety of other Asians. Like Hispanics, they have come for relief from poverty and oppression. Many are survivors living with keen self-preservation instincts. Learning about self-government, voluntary payment of taxes, school attendance, and helpful rather than punitive policemen is almost more than they can handle.

But the Hispanics and Asians don't participate in normal political processes. Their voting registration rate is low and voting record even lower. They conduct an underground economy and employment market that scarcely resembles the legally sanctioned systems. Settled into ethnic communities with deteriorating schools and increasing crime rates, they are seldom heard in government councils. A state assemblyperson in south Los Angeles struggles to get consensus from his people, who seldom speak to government. When this group is juxtaposed to the politically entrenched, whose problems get addressed? But the well-entrenched happen to be the group over 55, the largest voting bloc in the state. This group votes against schools, highways, welfare, workers compensation benefits, and most taxes generally. But it votes for security measures, health care for the aging, and smaller government. Thus a head-on collision of interest is coming when the immigrant groups become fully participating in California political life. If the minority aged demanded and could get what white anglos over 65 assume is their due, health and social services would be swamped, even drown. The eventual solution will begin when self-interests of the older citizen are outvoted by younger and minority groups or when the over-55-age group agrees to encumber itself with more obligations for the care of people with greater needs.

California may be a model for other states and cities with large populations of immigrants. Particularly affected are sunbelt states and areas where employment is available. From this day forward, whenever the problems of the aging are addressed, it will always be in relation to the needs of other groups entering the main stream of American life. Let's summarize pertinent statistics furnished by our government through its census studies:

• 12 percent of the US population is over 65 years of age. The over-65 group has grown 14 percent since 1980. The under-65 group has grown 5 percent during the same period. About 2.2 million people turn 65 every year.

• The group over 85 years of age has grown 22 times since 1900. Life expectancy has increased 28 years since 1900.

• Women outnumber men in the ratio of 147 to 100 in the over-65 population. And this is the era of equal opportunity?

• By the year 2030, 21 percent of the population will be over 65, 65.6 million people.

• For those over 65, median net worth is about double the value for those under 65. In 1986 it was $32,700 for the under 65 and over $60,000 for those over 65. Inflation moves ever upward, changing these figures about 100 percent each ten years.

• 83 percent of homeowners over 65 have no mortgages.

• 7 percent of householders over 65 have a net worth of $250,000 or more. Your chances of becoming an "inflation millionaire" are better every year!

• Until the time of DRG (diagnostically related groups) health cost reimbursement, those over 65 accounted for 31 of all health-care expenses while they comprised but 12 percent of the population. In 1984 Medicare-Medicaid paid out 81 billion dollars. The first entire Eisenhower federal budget was about 65 billion dollars.

•The age group over 65 has more discretionary income than any other group—income not needed for necessities. But the same age group is at once the second poorest as well as the richest group in our country. Only the children of poverty stricken parents are poorer. But the very rich also tend to be quite old. In spite of the way we sometimes behave, 100 percent of us will leave our money behind when we die!

Few politicians will vote against the basic needs of an established, older voting bloc. But from now on they will be in competition for shortening tax dollars in an inflationary economy. The older establishment, like establishments before them, may become disestablished by effective competition. They are presently the "limelight" group, but the light is being redirected to other critical problems. So it has been with previous establishments who once dominated social and public interest—the church, education, big business, the military complex, and unions. The next establishment may the environment and the people who are charged with caring for it. Seniors will adapt to aging with more difficulty in the future and their needs become relatively less important in the political arena.

The distilled message of these truths and myths of aging is that much folklore has arisen about life in later years. Only recently has gerontology become a well-disciplined science, with graduate schools and research institutes dispelling the myths we know. As a result we will do well if we carefully reconsider much of the lore so commonly believed about aging. A lot of sorting and verifying is yet to be done. Don't let commonly held notions about aging impose limits upon you because they are accepted as truth. Furthermore, I know of no biblical statement that declares a limit on what you can become by the grace of God. The timeless truths of Scripture challenge us yet.

References

1. The statistics developed in this chapter are based upon data furnished by the U.S. Bureau of the Census and the U.S. National Center for Health Statistics. A helpful brochure available from the American Association of Retired Persons, Program Resources Dept., Washington, D.C. was compiled by Donald G. Fowles and published in 1988.
2. Holmes, Thomas H. and Rahe, R., "Stress Rating Scale," in *Journal of Psychosomatic Research*, 1967, Vol. 2, p. 216.
3. Ahlem, Lloyd H. *Do I Have To Be Me?* (Ventura, California: Regal Books, 1974).
4. This outline suggested by Mark Lee, president emeritus of Simpson College, in an address in Turlock, California, July 1989.
5. Mead, Frank S., *The Encyclopedia of Religious Quotations*, (Old Tappan, New Jersey: Spire Books, 1976).
6. Ibid.
7. Ibid.
8. Miller, Keith, *A Hunger for Healing*, (San Francisco: Harper Collins, 1991).
9. Mead, Frank S., *The Encyclopedia of Religious Quotations*, (Old Tappan, New Jersey: Spire Books, 1976).
10. Lewis, C. S., *The Great Divorce*, (Toronto: Macmillan Co., 1946).
11. The ideas on politics and economics of aging and California as a third world state are developed by Dan Walters in *The New California: Facing the 21st Century* (Sacramento, California: Journal Press, 1986).

Questions for Discussion

1. Describe your own community as a political and economic

milieu and estimate what this means for aging people, for your church, and for future generations.
2. What is a Christian response likely be in caring for the old, who are at once, the poorest and the richest group of people in America?
3. How do you respond to the competing needs of the aging, the poor, and the underprivileged? State your present Christian position on caring for the needs of people and what that position implies for your personal commitment of time and focus of activity.

THREE

Aptitudes Maintained Through Aging

Brain rot!" muttered Margaret as she went out the door to the post office. She forgot to pick up the letters she wanted to mail. She returned to the house, got the mail, and went back to the car. "Double brain rot!" she shouted. She had left her car keys on the kitchen table while she picked up the letters. She retrieved the keys and tried to unlock the car door. "Triple brain rot! I've got the wrong keys! What's my old head up to?"

At 80 years she fretted that age was giving her fits. More likely she was trying to remember too many things at once. If you live long, will your brain deteriorate? The idea is not supported by current research. A recent study by the National Institute for Aging using brain scan techniques showed that healthy men in their eighties have brains as active and useful as men in their twenties and thirties. If that's true, why are we persuaded that brains fail with age?

The idea that age produces senility is a self-fulfilling prophecy according to experts in geriatrics. Senility is a disease symptom, not a normal development in advanced years. Merion Perimutter, in her book on memory and aging, says that older people exaggerate their memory losses because they have awaited them with dread. Warner Shaie, a leading researcher on the subject, believes that if older people reject the stereotype of "old and dull" they are likely to maintain better functioning. John Horn, psychologist at University of Denver, believes that problem-solving and judgmental reasoning do not decline but increase through the life span. Jerry Avorn of Harvard Medical School's Division on Aging believes that minor deficits in certain types of ability are not so much impairments as nuisances. There may be some loss in the ability to recognize abstract patterns and relationships, but these are not critical to exercising wisdom.

People who maintain their abilities most fully usually do three things:

1) Stay active socially. People who become recluses in older age do not keep the intellect stimulated. Women, the widowed, and the poorly educated who spend life alone suffer most.

2) Keep up their intellectual interests. Well-educated people who keep abreast of their fields increase their knowledge and judgmental acuity as they age. Floyd Bloom at the Scripps Clinic in La Jolla, California, suggests that the brain is changing every day, adding and subtracting brain cells, connections between cells, and strengthening and weakening connections. Through learning, a person may add billions of connections in the higher learning centers. So much is being discovered about the brain that neuroscience is plunging ahead in basic research. In 1969, the Society for Neuroscience was formed with 500 members. Today it exceeds 12,000. A scientific revolution wrenching us loose from our assumed understandings is under way.

3) Have flexible personalities. They tolerate ambiguities, enjoy new experiences, find conflicting-ideas puzzles to enjoy, not stresses to resolve. They do not become victims of rigid, doctrinaire thought systems. When I was first studying mental ability we were told that the brain is not a muscle that strengthens with use, but that you were born with an inherited ability that remains constant. Now we teach the opposite. Warner Shaie's experiments indicate that the "use it or lose it" idea is credible. Growth of intellect continues, although at a slower rate in later years. It does not significantly decline, except as a part of disease.

The long list of studies showing that intellect declined with age was biased in at least three ways. First, younger subjects were compared with older ones without correcting for educational opportunity. Younger people likely received a post-high-school education. Older people most often ended training at grade-school levels. This would explain a lot of difference in intellectual stimulation and acquisition of information, the stuff of which abstract intelligence is comprised. Second, various kinds of intelligence were not considered. Most tests contain questions measuring only abstract reasoning power, which shows slight decline with age. But more useful kinds of intellect—such as creativity and judgmental acuity—are usually not measured by standardized tests at all. Third, with age comes vulnerability to disease. Many studies are not so much measures of decline as they are measures of increase in disease that affect mental acuity. When disease is eliminated, the differences between younger and older groups disappear.

I think there are at least four kinds of ability that do not decline with age. More likely they increase. Because the body loses flexibility and strength and we camp longer in doctor's offices it is easy to think our aptitudes are getting away from us. Because bones don't flex like willow sticks, or we forget where the light switch is in a dark bathroom doesn't mean we can't comprehend new discoveries in astronomy. It just means we have had a few birthdays—nothing more. Consider the following abilities:

1) Lingual—intellectual capacity. If the brain suffers no serious organic damage, it will function well into advanced years. Daniel Goleman, in the New York Times, summarized research on aging brains and suggested that old people have greater ability to wax eloquently, to say the same thing in numerous ways. They have evocative fluency, better than young people similarly studied. Word usage is more varied and subtler meanings expressed.

About 90 percent of all seniors will keep their intellectual powers until weeks or even hours before death. My mother was an example. She lived her last 18 months in a nursing home. One Friday afternoon I visited her to say that we were going to our cabin in the mountains for the weekend. "Have a great time!" she responded. "See you on Monday." By the time we arrived at the cabin, she had expired, a victim of congestive heart failure. But she was fully lucid within one hour of death. She is more the normal case than the exception.

I have noticed on IQ tests, such as the Wechsler, that if an adjustment is made for slower speed of response, mental acuity remains constant. Unfortunately, some think that loss of speed is the same as loss of quality of intellect. But the mind processes information a little more slowly in age and impatient observers assume intellectual quality has suffered.

Actually, the opposite may be true. Older people have more information to sort through to make a good response to a test question. All the possible answers appear to be right in varying degrees, increasing the chances an astute mind will choose the wrong one. Some tests make brighter people look bad because these people have too many reference points against which to consider an answer. Such tests are widely used in educational institutions. Many people believe abilities decline with age because of death of brain cells. Marion Diamond of the University of California tried to track down the source of this myth and could find no studies bearing it out. Her own studies suggest that while there is some loss in age, the greatest decrease in is in early life and losses are insignificant later on.

I think of an 85-year-old woman who made a list of objectives for the next ten years of her life a day before she died. You can bet safely she had little intellectual loss in her later years. She was a voracious reader, educating herself in the subjects of politics, nutrition, and biblical theology. A Sunday school teacher for more than 40 years, she was keenly interested in these topics. In the retirement center where she lived, people scrambled to get to her table at dinner because she was such a stimulating conversationalist. When she died, we lost our living encyclopedia.

2) Creativity. In the 1950s, an intense interest in creative aptitude began—tied to our concern for national security and the improvement of education. I was a doctoral student in those days and got thoroughly immersed in the research produced. A prominent name in the field was J. P. Guilford at the University of Southern California.[1] He believed that creativity was a cumulative aptitude that developed with age and with creative activity. Furthermore, creativity was not confined to artistic fields, but expressed itself wherever inventiveness could be manifest. Everyone had some of it—creative scientists, mechanics, carpenters, homemakers, and teachers.

Studies show little correlation between creativity and IQ in people of average or greater verbal ability. In Lewis Terman's *Genetic Studies of Genius*[2] none of the people with extremely high IQ was very creative. Not one produced a significant work of art or literature or developed a major technical advance. Instead, they were mental "jacks of all trades," absorbed by books, understanding a lot about everything, and performing unusually in nothing. They were bookish, well-educated, intellectual blotters who absorbed information exceedingly well and entered professional occupations. Though their IQs were all in the top one percent of the population, creativity was not correspondingly present.

If creativity advances with age and stimulation we should find highly creative people among the elderly. Furthermore, we should be providing rich and stimulating environments for them. But unfortunately, school and society are great levelers and squelchers of creative production. Both our educational and business institutions value conformity and right answers more than feisty personalities and creative people. Sweet dullards don't upset teachers and managers half as much and are tolerated endlessly. A documentary on Walt Disney said that he was fired from a newspaper advertising job for not following the guidelines for advertising copy and for showing little promise for advancement. Einstein had difficulty passing math tests for entrance to the university. Churchill failed exams for entrance to the infantry and his father despaired for his future. Conformist thinkers seldom dent history!

I had a friend who survived school with a terrible attendance record and minimal grades. He got into a university where he proved a very average engineering student. He never let high grades get in the way of his inventiveness. Only a wise uncle kept him from dropping out numerous times, while paying his tuition to keep him at his studies. In his eighties, my friend got his one-hundred-twenty-first patent. He had figured out a way to significantly reduce the amount of water necessary to cool a nuclear reaction. Physicists and ecologists who were concerned by the warm water's effect upon the environment were immediately interested. In recognition of his achievements, his alma mater offered him an honorary degree. But when the university would not guarantee a parking place at commencement, he refused. Instead, I had the pleasure of conferring a doctorate for his work in thermodynamics and for his contributions to our science program at North Park College. He was too creative to be very much of a book worm, but the value of his ideas will add to physics books for years to come.

I believe retired people may have our most creative minds. They may not have had opportunity to be inventive but it is time they did. Research indicates that creativity increases until the later 70s, and then the examiners may have run out older people to test or graduate students to test them. Mandatory retirement at 65 shunts away the most able people in our schools and businesses.

3) Capacity for play. In *Christians At Play*,[3] Robert K. Johnston says, "From Augustine to the present day, Christians have often been suspicious of play. 'Work for the Night Is Coming' has been our motto. But Christians today are rediscovering the need to play. In a world in which work gravitates toward the extremes of ulcers and boredom, and at a time when the richness of play is being made increasingly available, Christian theology is being challenged to reassess its suspicions concerning play." Johnston's text finds solid ground between the traditional work ethic and the hedonistic obsessions of twentieth-century Americans at play. According to

Johnston, there is a shape for human life which maintains crucial balance between work and play.

Play is self-regenerative. As such it is absolutely necessary. It is not the play of porpoises and chimpanzees, but celebrative activity of minds and emotions seeking regeneration and renewal. It adds joy and elasticity to the mind. It is not just amusement, where the brain is turned off by banal stimuli. Pure amusement can be an anesthetizing activity that dulls intellect and moral sensitivity. To muse is to think. To amuse is to negate thought. To play is to celebrate and renew one's spirit.

Play has an effect something like sleep. If we don't get it we go bonkers. I remember studies of college students wired to electroencephalographs so their brain waves could be charted while they slept. When the brain wave tracing indicated they were dreaming, they were awakened, asked what they were dreaming about and allowed to go back to sleep. Every dream was interrupted similarly. After ten days they were cranky and tired, openly hostile to the examiners. It was as if they had not slept at all. Play is like that. If we are deprived of it or addicted to work, we become irritable and difficult. If we learn to play productively we are self-renewing people and much easier to endure. I heard about a workaholic manager of a very large company who was forced to retire. When he left, the company threw a tremendous retirement party, but they didn't invite the retiring manager. The employees were so happy to see him go they didn't want to spoil his leaving with his presence!

Play is non-physical, fantasy recreation. For seniors it is no longer flag football on a Sunday afternoon. Instead, it is applying the mind to wholesome fantasies that stimulate creative thought. It is recasting old ideas into new settings. It is an earned, extended sabbatical for those in advanced years. We mostly think of the sabbath as a spiritual function rather than a recreative one. But the sabbath predated Jewish worship and may have had little to do with religion at its inception. The sabbath was a renewal experience first. This is the idea behind the sabbatical leaves given to professors who have found that knowledge keeps about as well as fish. Teachers, especially, need to prevent dullness from making them toxic to their students. I think Henry Ward Beecher had the idea straight when he said, "God's altar stands from Sunday to Sunday, and the seventh day is no more for religion than any other—it is for rest. The whole seven are for religion, and one of them for rest, for instruction, for social worship, for gaining strength for the other six."

As our years extend, longer periods of renewal are not luxuries, but necessities. A pastor friend, just now retiring, plans to spend one full year reading. Not that he will ever apply his learning extensively; he just wants to be refreshed. In contrast, I know an old gentleman who will not play at anything. He worked all his life and feels guilty about retirement. He will not play because he can't quench the idea that he hasn't earned the right to his free time. So he sits and stews or wanders the community, deteriorating in health and mind. I can't believe the creator had this in mind for older people.

Since play is closely related to creative activity, capacity for play is ever growing. Later years should be filled with play and the renewal of creative juices. Furthermore, retirement centers and programs should be filled with creative activity and very little concerned with amusement. Robert Gordis says, ". . . joy is God's categorical imperative for man, not in any anemic or spiritualized sense, but rather as a full-blooded and tangible experience, expressing itself in the play of the body, and the activity of the mind, the contemplation of nature and pleasures of love."[4]

4) Capacity for spiritual development. The Bible says nothing about limits on our spiritual growth, unlike our other capacities. Apparently, limits are self-imposed. Instead, the Bible challenges us with far-reaching possibilities. I recall a senior-high-school camp speaker whose adventurous career as a Christian businessman demonstrated faith. "If I could do it again," he stressed, "I would trust more, dare more, and fear less. Though I achieved things I never thought I would, I have lived my life short-changing myself by not believing enough about God's ability." Limits, apparently, are self-imposed.

James 1:5 says, "If any of you lack wisdom, let him ask of God, that giveth to all men liberally, and upbraideth not; and it shall be given him." John 14:27 makes a wonderful promise: "Peace I leave with you, my peace I give unto you: not as the world giveth, give I unto you. Let not your hear be troubled, neither let it be afraid."

Peace and wisdom are but two examples of promises made to believers. The Scriptures harbor no evidence there is a ceiling on what we can become spiritually. Perhaps declining physical abilities impel us to trust and search out qualities of the Spirit. We are not very old when we learn that we are flesh—fallen and failing people. If aging has a purpose, it must be to help see more clearly the spiritual reality of life and the promise of life beyond. If the only purpose of aging is to burn our youthful resources, then we can join the mobs of people who serve the cult of youth.

But what spiritual possibilities are there for someone rendered incapable—wrecked by Alzheimer's disease or dementia? Are they in a spiritual no-man's land? What about the seriously retarded, whose reasoning is nil? I think of a friend—once a gifted pastor, with keen spiritual insight. Now, when I visit, barely a flicker of recognition suggests he knows me. Yet when his wife draws him to her side and repeats benedictions with which he often blessed his congregations, he settles into peace and his restlessness abates. It is as if God specially comes to him in that moment and soothes his spirit.

Or I think of my father, who died of brain cancer at age 66. In his last days words were useless. When we tried to talk he made signs indicating he was ready for heaven and planned to be there soon. He short cut any thought of going home—except to indicate he was going to his heavenly home. Now I respond to people who seem to be without intellect as if the last sensitivity was awareness of God. To my father I would say a familiar, simple prayer close to his ear. One night he passed away, and my last words to his failing cancer-ridden mind were words of a benediction he often used as pastor to those who were critically ill. I trusted God that such words would now bless him.

I stopped at the bedside of a friend who had no perceivable awareness I was there. "No use talking to him," his brother said resignedly. "He won't get it." I was visibly repelled by his words. But I stroked my friend's arm and prayed for him anyway, for I am convinced we abort ministry to the incapacitated much too early. The Spirit has ways of reaching us the intellect has little capacity to understand.

I also believe that older people are capable of ministry until their last hours. The form of ministry may not be very active, but it is nonetheless highly functional. It is the ministry of intercession. Seniors have the time. With opportunity, awareness, and knowledge from years of discipleship, seniors can become powerful intercessors. The persuasive prayer of seniors will prod spiritual growth and defuse volatile problems better than any number of up-to-date, snappy programs.

I recently met with a young man who was deeply involved in pastoral training in eastern Europe. He was persuaded that Christian faith has been preserved by the grandmothers of Russia. These older people had lost their own children to atheistic Marxism, but serving as caretakers for their grandchildren, had taught them vital elements of the Gospel. Grandparents were too old for re-education by the state, or so thought the politicians. So they were released to educate a whole generation of youngsters who will bring spiritual life to Eastern Europe again. Seniors with their wisdom and knowledge of prayer are our most needed church resource.

References

1. Guilford, J.P., *The Nature of Human Intelligence* (New York, McGraw-Hill, 1967).
2. Terman, L.M., *Genetic Studies of Genius, Vol. 1* (Stanford, California, Stanford University Press, 1925).
3. Johnston, Robert K. *Christians at Play* (Grand Rapids, Michigan, Williams B. Erdmans Co., 1983).
4. Gordis, Robert, *Koholeth. . . .The Man and His World* (New York, Shocken Books, 1968), p. 131.

Questions for Discussion

1. Think back to about the sixth grade. Recall the students in your class in school. Rank them in school ability, including yourself. How many were there and what number were you? This is a fairly good indicator of your IQ as you applied it.
2. How many books have you read in the last five years? What intellectual stimulation have you pursued for its own sake?
3. What creative or unusual activities do you like? Are you an artist? Punster? Musician? Maker of gimmicks and gadgets? Do you itch mentally? Describe your favorite intellectual activity.
4. Do you agree or disagree with the idea that there are aptitudes that don't decline with age. Support your argument and describe why you take the position you do.

FOUR

Transitions in Aging

It was a beautiful, balmy day—warm under azure skies and gentle breezes. "Great day for a holiday!" announced Father Ming. "I think we'll head for the beach and forget all the hassle going on in our country for a few hours." So the Ming family picked up picnic baskets, umbrellas, a radio, their cash assets, and legal papers and headed for the shores of the China Sea. While the war was still a hundred miles away, no one left any assets at home unguarded. The Ming children—along with a teenage governess—romped in the sand, and war was all but forgotten. But shortly the radio interrupted with jarring news. The Tet offensive had begun and was moving fast in the direction of the Ming home. The Mings scrambled to get things together, jumped in their station wagon, and raced for home.

A few miles short of their town, the thunder of canons could be heard and jets were screaming low overhead. The Mings were abruptly halted at a road block and turned back. "But where will we go?" worried a little Ming youngster. "To the airport!" shouted father, "Down in Saigon." "But then where?" continued the children. "Anywhere that is safe that will take us in!" retorted Father. "But where will our governess go?" the children inquired. "She'll go with us. She can't get home and her town has been overrun!" The Ming family's connections in government were about to pay off. Relatives in America had also been urging their flight. They got reservations via Hong Kong to Canada and then to the United States. They were one of the few intact families to get out in the midst of conflict. But with them was a most devastated governess—now shuttled halfway across the world without being able to tell her family what had happened or where she was. She was only sixteen years of age, with no idea of what her choices and chances might be, except to go along with the Mings.

The governess, whom we dubbed Sherri, sat with me over coffee one Saturday afternoon and spoke freely about her wrenching experience. She was a waitress in one of our centers and lived with a local family. Her English was promisingly good and she had completed high school. Seven years had passed, but not a word from her family had reached her. She wrote hundreds of letters but had no way of knowing if they were getting through. As we talked, she spoke of being jerked out of her country, having all family ties torn up, struggling with English, going for days without a cent of cash, and wondering who would feed her next. I could imagine no more volcanic change for anyone than this young woman had endured. Then she asked a perceptive question, "Do you think these old people felt like I did when I had to leave my home? I bet they missed their families, too, if they came a long way. Did they get a chance to say goodbye? Did they have to leave lots of things behind—like friends and homes and belongings? I never got to tell anyone anything in Vietnam; I disappeared! My family must have thought I was dead. Everything ended for me but I didn't get to end anything. I wonder if they think I was impolite for leaving without telling them. I wonder what my mother really thinks of me. It all happened so quickly!" Sherri worked for us for seven years. Then she married and now has two beautiful children. She also has been able to exchange mail with her mother, but her father and brother disappeared in the war. Family connections have been partly reestablished. And no, they didn't think ill of her for leaving in such a hurry. Her life was likely spared by the Ming family, who provided connections for a successful escape.

Sherri's story reminded me of a line from T.S. Eliot in "Little Gidding."[1] "What we call the beginning is often the end. And to make an end is to make a beginning. The end is where we start from." As Sherri and I compared the changes for retired people with the upheaval in her life, we realized that we don't begin a new phase in life very well without first closing off present commitments and parting with people and places. We need parties, protocol, and ceremonies to finish one stage of life so we can begin another. We don't start anything new until we make an end of the present.

Then I remembered the most convulsive change I imposed on my family. We left university teaching in California to assume a college presidency in Illinois. Our five children had no idea what was in store for them. We changed geography, climate, schools, friends, church, social structures, behavioral expectations, vacation places, summer camps, and the house we would live in. It was years before I realized how pervasive the effect would be. Before we left we were the recipients of parties, a church blessing, last visits to relatives, one more vacation in the mountains, a new car, and endless talk. We sold the house, the boat, a car, and had a garage sale dispossessing us of most of our familiar trinkets. People were kinder than they needed to be and we were in high spirits from all the attention. But limbo was just ahead; confusion shrouded by all the well wishes of friends. The gleam of adventure and promise of new horizons would soon yield to struggling in no-man's land. Said Zen: "After the enlightenment, the laundry!"

One senior said it well, "When I fulfilled my dream of retiring and moving to the Pacific Northwest, I thought I would end the hassles of work and enjoy the ease earned by my labor. But it was more like the upheaval I went through when I was drafted into the army in 1942 with only two weeks notice." The number and intensity of normal transitions is greater in retirements than in other phases of life, barring natural disaster or war. Here is what happens:

Detachment: People you once worked with are seldom seen any more. If you have not planned for new people to replace your working friends you will feel isolated and lost. Some folks wisely make new friends who will become their peers after they stop working, sorting out who they will enjoy and who will be of no interest to them. Then they will have a congenial group to receive them.

Repositioning: At work there are bosses and workers, supervisors and staff members, all arranged in pecking orders. Our place in this system tells us who we are and where we belong. But with retirement, we lose position and rank. We are only people making their way in a new pecking order. Skills necessary to live in this new system—which is largely social—can be very different from skills that gave us status in the job. The result is disorientation and uncertainty. I knew a college administrator, replaced by a new president's personal colleague. When my friend rejoined the faculty he could not stop pontificating. Deference to his position was lost. Neither did his former power over people give him clout in his department. He spent several miserable years reprogramming his brain to learn a new set of rules and relational skills.

Disorientation: As long as we work, we plan for progress in a career. We identify goals, such as position or income, by which to steer a course. But in retirement, these symbols and achievements only tell us where we were. As one retired friend asked, "Do I save money now or do I spend what I have saved? Do I turn my den back into a garage? Am I a professional or a handyman? I am neither going up in my profession, nor sideways. I don't know my navigation points anymore!"

Memory loves to relish and embellish what we once were. Most friends will let us tell them about it—once or twice, but not more. We must close off old experiences and can't begin something new until we do. A retired general left one of our facilities after a very short stay. Staff and residents wouldn't take his orders. He was no general to them; just another resident who wanted lordship forever.

Disconfirmation: At career's end we polish our past. Our minds cloud failure and exaggerate success. But if we lived without sound reasons for our work, we may be plagued by self-doubt. I picked up a golf game with a retired liquor salesperson one day. He spent two hours compulsively telling me, a total stranger, why he was justified spending a lifetime peddling booze. I'm glad I've been spared a similar need. He had made his mark selling a product harmful to people and resulting disconfirmations of himself possessed him.

As we complete our endings to make beginnings we enter the neutral zone. Old connections are gone, new ones not yet established. Its a no-man's land, emotionally; chaotic, uncertain, lonely—except for a few friends who may sense our needs. One gentleman retired and moved in with his children, but complained for weeks that he didn't know where he was. He must have anticipated his confusion because he didn't sell his home a hundred miles away. Back and forth he journeyed; not that he had anything to do when he got there. But touching familiar places helped him. In a year he found a woman he courted with more enthusiasm than she returned. But she gave him a sense of belonging in his new place. Meanwhile, his children had no idea why he felt so lost and were miffed at his inability to settle in. After all, they were his kids and had invited him to join them.

What do we feel in the neutral zone? Numbness, immobilization, paralysis of the will. "My get up and go got up and went," lamented one retiree. "Can't unpack my boxes. I keep writing my old phone number at new banks and stores." But such chaos may be necessary. A psychiatrist once said we all need the "productive work of worry" in the neutral zone. The mind must churn awhile before it can think usefully. The musings of a fumbling mind gives the heart a chance to settle. William Bridges cites Mircea Eliade in *The Sacred and the Profane*[2] as saying: "The symbolic return to chaos is indispensable to any new creation." You may not know if you are going to be crazy or enlightened; it all feels the same.

The neutral zone experience confirms that life is not neatly organized into well-defined stages. Instead, life is ebb and flow, side steps, restarts and false starts, complete changes in field of work, sudden catapults into leadership, quick declines to lesser posts, sudden career endings. There are special opportunities in the neutral times, however. With fewer, firm time or production commitments, we can rethink what we truly want to have happen to us. Or we can spend healthy time in reflection. These are the wildernesses of life, well-known to Jesus and the Apostles John and Paul. The Israelites wandered forty years before entering the promised land. A long desert experience prepared Moses for leading his people out of Egypt.

These experiences are not lost, extended weekends. If we expose ourselves to the voice of God through his Word, meditation, and prayer, they may be highly regenerative times. Anxious people flail desperately to shorten them by flurries of activity. But their efforts muddle thinking and produce bad decisions. It is a time for intuition, not for compulsive economic moves or personal commitments. At the end of no-man's land we come to the beginning. Just as Good Friday was the end of an old spiritual economy, so Easter was the beginning of grace. Tumult and death marked the close of an era. In the three days between death and resurrection, those closest to the salvation drama appeared to have no clue as to what would happen. Some tried to return to old occupations, some hid away, some remained in limbo. But Easter dawned and resurrection changed the lives of these men forever.

John Galsworthy said it correctly, "The beginnings of all human undertakings are messy."[3] There is no such thing as a smooth start. If there was, we would only be repeating something we have done before. Any new start is creative activity to which chaos and clutter is essential. We long for external clues, for bench marks, for known navigation points to tell us where we are headed. One of the astronauts venturing to the moon stated that the space ship was off course 95 percent of the time. Exploration and adventure is a series of corrections for error. Bridges says that in archaic cultures, the myths of the world are recited over sick people.[4] Such myths become the road signs into the unknown. In more Christian terms, the success of our pilgrimage is dependent upon the quality of our personal acquaintance with God's revelation and our ability to live by faith.

Here are some helps for the beginnings at the end of our neutral zones.

• Any start is a good start. All starts are messy. Stop getting ready and get moving. Vehicles steer more easily than those at dead stop. End the tears—postpone further grief. Grab whatever presents itself as a handle on the situation, even if it is the middle of the problem and you must work both ways from there.

• Identify the final picture of your dream. Know what that picture looks like so when you come to it you will recognize it. You must be as realistic as possible. Some people realize their dreams and can't tell they have arrived. But don't become so enamored with your goal you can't get untangled from messy ways of getting there. Dreams can be escape devices, diverting us to fantasy. Plow ahead knowing the plowshare is going to stick on a stump or two.

• Move in small, comprehendable steps. Clear up the little things from time to time. The task is clearer as the trash is whisked away. Don't attack the entire problem at once. Tackle a piece of the job that fits your capacity to work worry free. If you stew too much you have not broken the job down into small enough tasks. Then look up from time to time to see the whole of it.

• Resist the temptation to believe there is a simple solution, if it could only be found. Plenty of siren songs are sung over complex problems—sung by people who yearn for just the right program or leader to take them out of their confusion. Plenty of saints are willing to fold their hands and let their problems be solved supernaturally when God has already provided other means to do it simply, if not without effort.

• Get going and double your rate of failure. Such was the advice given by Mr. Watson, founder of IBM. If your failure rate is doubled by sincere and discerning effort, the success rate will more than double. We can trash many of the wrong answers, but we are looking for only one solution.

• Do not refer to a committee for further study, even if the committee is your family. Committees work well at the onset of transitions provided they are limited to generating ideas. Individuals generate intuitions more than groups. Good intuition is what is necessary when information is sketchy, when risk is high, and when leadership is required.

• Define this time of your life positively. Retirement is transition, not termination. A woman at age 65 has an average of 21 years left. A man at 65 has about 16. If you reach 75, a woman could live 14 more years, and a man almost as much. You will do a lot of something after age 65. Christians may retire, but they never lose their calling. So plan to participate actively in a great mission.

• Envision you first days of retirement so they are not so different from your last days at work. Remember that your plan becomes the prophecy that determines the pattern for your remaining years. Without a plan, trivia will fill your hours and crowd you as much as your employment did, and often with as much stress. A friend of mine retired without clear plans and was asked what he was doing with his time. "Well..." he replied. "I don't know, but it takes all day!"

• Plan on being active. If you don't, you will sleep late, watch too much TV, and take naps. Inactivity creates health problems. Exercise to stay flexible. Good conditioning is more important than ever.

• Plan for a new time in relationship with your spouse. Can you stand your mate all day? Can your mate stand you? A busy executive retired and came home to stay. He assumed full command of the household, just as he had done at the office. It was only a short while until his wife told him she would either retire, too, or divorce him. He got the message. As one woman put it to her husband, "I married you for better or worse, but not for lunch. Now get off to your country club for a while."

If both spouses have been working, two may be retiring—not just one. So you go through withdrawal and adjustment together. No man's land can be tough going if you are fumbling through, looking to your spouse for support and stability. Consider retiring at different times. This may ease a financial burden as well as managing one adjustment at a time. If you find yourself snapping and chewing at each other, consider a helpful formula for communicating developed by H. Norman Wright[5]—to which I have added minor points:

1) We will express our irritations with each other in loving specific ways rather than holding or using them as weapons or reasons for retaliation.

2) We will not exaggerate our gripes. We will avoid the use of

"always, all the time, you never, everyone."

3) We will stick to specifics and not expand the agenda during the discussion.

4) We will assume responsibility for control of the intensity and emotional level of the arguments.

5) We will have "time outs" in any difficult argument but we will not run away from each other during an argument.

6) We will complete any argument by sundown, never going to sleep angry.

7) We will listen to each other well enough so as to be able to accurately restate the other's concern.

8) We will not rehearse the other person's failures during the course of the discussion.

9) Outside interferences will be avoided, such as radio, TV, books, and chores. Our discussions will be private.

10) We will share the time available for discussion and will not interrupt each other. Transitions are periods for healthy discussions, not wrangling arguments. They are times when tentative thoughts, possibilities, "what if" kinds of ideas, and "what would happen if" types of statements can be made. But they must be made in the comfort of trusting relationships. When the transition is over, happy times can result.

References

1. Eliot, T.S. *Four Quartets* (New York, Harcourt-Brace, 1943), p. 38.
2. Eliade, Mircea, *Myths. Dreams. and Mysteries*, Translated by Philip Mairet (New York, Harper and Row, 1967), p. 80.
3. Galsworthy, John, *Over the River* (London: Wm. Heineman,1933), p. 4.
4. Bridges, William, *Transitions: Making Sense of Life's Changes* (Reading, Massachuchettts, Addison-Wesley Publishing Co., 1980).
5. Wright, H. Norman, *More Communication For Your Marriage*, (Ventura, California: Regal Books, 1987), pp.113-115.

Questions for Discussion

1. Describe the most troublesome change you have had to make in your life. As you look back, can you identify with the three stages discussed in this chapter?
2. What emotions did you feel as you went through each stage? Did you feel surprised by any of your emotions? Did anyone make you feel bad about the way you felt?
3. Who or what helped you most during your transition? How will you approach the next big move in your life?

4. How can you help another going through a major change in life? Do you consider helping to be an individual responsibility or the responsibility of the church, local government, or other service?

FIVE

Stresses and Uplifts in Retirement

Moving out of a career and into retirement is normally one of life's largest changes. Even if the transition is well planned, anticipated enthusiastically, and seen as an economic way of rearranging life, pain pervades. While we are firm believers in the value of the lifestyle and care retirement facilities provide, the fact remains that normal high-stress events occur increasingly in advanced years, wherever home may be. In an informal poll of residents in continuing care facilities, several stress factors were mentioned repeatedly.[1] Below is a list of those stresses, followed by uplifts we also discovered.

Stress Factors

- Making the decision to retire and enter a retirement facility, a decision often accompanied by mixed and competing feelings.
- Ridding oneself of possessions to live in smaller and newer facilities. Attachments have been formed to valued items, sometimes acquired over many years.
- Economic repositioning. Ending work and its regular paycheck, accepting a pension, getting Social Security, selling assets, withdrawing funds from long-established savings programs. Rewriting wills and establishing trusts.
- Walking out of one's home for the last time, entering a new place to live, and feeling totally unfamiliar with surroundings. A momentary but potent emotional experience.
- Changes in health, extended illnesses, reduced physical capacity. Experiencing the fact that multiple chronic conditions are more frequent past age 75.
- Abrupt moves to health-care centers such as nursing homes

or extended care facilities. Loss of self-choice in this process is most painful.

• Loss of spouse. Ratios of women to men in retirement facilities are often 3 or 4 to 1. The loss is often anticipated and grieving done in advance. The loss seems to be less stressful than being forced to enter health-care facilities. But personal and social life changes immensely.

• Role reversals with children or care-givers. Decision-making surrendered to others, especially children. May be necessary and helpful, but very stressful.

• Reconsideration of decisions. Having made a large number of high impact decisions in a short time, temptations are present to rethink them. A few undo their decisions and must go through these stressful events a second time, which is often more difficult than the first time.

Uplifts

• Making new friends and establishing new relationships. Most retirees have more time for fun and socializing than ever. Most residents report that new acquaintances more than make up for associations they have lost. Most also overestimated the stress of leaving friends behind and underestimated the fun of finding new ones.

• Improved health and diet. In retirement centers, with supervised menus, most residents eat better than they did at home. Singles, particularly, have often neglected good nutrition and show marked improvement in general health. Men find there may be better cooks than their wives were before retirement.

• Release from troublesome chores. No gutters to clean, windows to wash, painting to be done, appliances to fix, roofs to sweep, snow to shovel, or furnaces to stoke. Freedom to focus on stimulating activities.

• Simplified economic management. If good estate planning and economic repositioning has been done, money worries are reduced. Most older people underestimate their net worth. Many can make moves that increase income and enhance security.

• Healthy dependence on others. Some dependence is self-limiting. So is some independence. With guidance, an optimum value can be achieved that liberates the retiree and preserves independence. But it is possible to buy so much assistance that well-being is reduced. Thus guidance to an optimum value is necessary. For example, one can buy food, transportation, and excess health care to the point that exercise ceases, overeating becomes a hobby, and emotional release is found in too many visits to the doctor's office.

- Luxury guilt. Many retirees move from older homes to newer facilities with conveniences they never knew before. With repositioned assets they can acquire facilities that would have been regarded as indulgent a decade or two earlier. But they enjoy their guilt! They may have moved up significantly in quality of life.
- Satisfying relationships with children and grandchildren. Time available enhances these relationships. But seeing children succeed in life, become mature, well-adjusted, and spiritually aware people is one of life's greatest joys.
- Focus of activities around aptitudes that don't decline with age, and release from responsibilities involving abilities that must decline with age. Or discovering aptitudes that have never been known before.

Responses to Change.

Since changes in advanced age are frequent and have considerable impact, seniors often respond with a great deal of feeling. In a helpful book, *Letting Go with Love*,[2] Nancy O'Connor suggests four responses to change. These are conservation, revolution, escape, and transcendence. Here are my definitions of these concepts in view of what I have seen occur:

Conservation: Some older people hang on to objects, ideas, and homes as if they were rejecting the future entirely. These items have been part of the good old days, and retirees feel compelled to keep them indefinitely. In public referendums they vote for the status quo. Realities of a changing world are not well faced.

I was a director of a bank in Chicago when we had to deal with an old immigrant in serious financial trouble. He owned and lived in a large apartment building, one in which he was first a renter, but later purchased as his fortunes improved. Now, with a very large equity and few other apartments occupied, he was unable to pay his remaining mortgage. We advised him how to refinance, sell, or improve the building to attract tenants. But he would hear none of it. This had been home since he immigrated in the 1920s and he was not going to change. We would have to repossess the building to secure payment and knew we would look like heels for throwing an old man out of his home. In the midst of our struggle, the man died. The building was sold and his heirs received a large sum. While the man was trying to save his place, his efforts were abetting the problem. Conservation has limited use in a fast-changing society and seniors, especially those who are highly dependent or passive, are likely to get stuck by this approach. Such folks are also likely to have fights with their children, who see the results of conserving too vigorously.

Revolution. Even as conservation is a form of denying changing reality, so revolution can be denial as well. I witnessed an eighty year old begin a venture with his grandson that required a large amount of cash. The grandson was a likeable young man, but without much business savvy. I think grandfather saw his own career beginning again. He had taken a similar venture years ago and made a small fortune for himself. Grandfather was revolting against passing years, living his life again in his grandson. The venture foundered, with grandfather and grandson differing sharply on management tactics and money uses. The boy is now much wiser and the grandfather much poorer. Similarly, we may see an older person throw him- or herself into work, repress grief, or deny change in health—revolting against the signs of their personal times. Such revolution may bring temporary relief from harsh realities, but it is seldom constructive.

Escape. Escaping from change is a tactic used frequently by either passive-aggressive people, or very dependent people. By passive-aggressive tactics, we mean the tendency to attack a problem, then let it drift into chaos by ignoring it. Similarly, very dependent people will let problems pile up and shove them off on others, particularly children. Then when children act to solve the problem, they are reproached for so doing. Thus passive-aggressive or dependent people escape having to do any real problem solving.

Escapists turn to chemical dependency and indulgence in food; they oversleep a great deal, or join a cult or religious group that offers simple release from stresses. I remember a woman who faced a diagnosis of cancer that required immediate treatment. But she missed many appointments with her physician, and when her sister hauled her off to the hospital, she was vilified as if she had caused the disease. Here we observed both dependency and passive-aggressive behavior. The patient could have lived a number of years, but died in a few months. Similarly I have seen seniors stay in their homes long beyond their abilities to manage for themselves. When children or relatives stepped in to prevent disaster, they were attacked—or the older people curled up emotionally and whined in dependency, complaining that their wishes were not being considered. Yet, if such people stay in their homes, they badger their friends for services and favors.

Transcendence. Transcendance is often a theological term, but here it means the capacity to see beyond the present grief or problem and come to a realistic solution. It means to think past one's feelings and inclinations to self-pity without denying the stresses involved. It means trusting one's spiritual resources to survive critical moments.

Occasionally. we see retirees reduced from vibrant living to dependency in a short time, proceeding from vigorous, outgoing lifestyles to near helplessness. I remember playing golf one Saturday with a healthy 86-year-old who became bedridden on Sunday. I used to kid him that he would be a great golfer if he ever got his maturity. A few days after our game, he grinned up at me and said, "I guess I'm getting my maturity now, and you sure guessed wrong as to what it would be like." But to him, maturity was a major step toward heaven. His capacity for transcendance of circumstances was such that he cheered his visitors far more than any cheered him. His last days were a model of maturity I would like to claim someday.

Having seen several hundred seniors face big decisions, I believe they group themselves into several types:

1) Default/inevitable choice. These are people who decide by not deciding. They do not get involved until it is too late, someone else has already decided for them, or all other alternatives have been eliminated. One such lady decided never to leave her home. With no plans for declining health or other significant changes, she waited until a stroke felled her and was carried to the hospital. From there she went to a nursing home where she died six months later.

2) The projected decision. The responsibility for a decision is laid upon another. The shift of responsibility may be overt or covert. I knew an old gentleman, nearly blind, who became acquainted with his neighbor only after living next door for many years. Then he consulted his neighbor about every detail of his life—most unusual because they had never met until this sudden intimacy came about. The neighbor listened carefully as a good neighbor would, and he found he was heir to half of the old gentleman's estate. But implicit in being an heir was responsibility for managing the older person's

affairs. When the neighbor realized how much he had become involved, he found us and we became the caretaker, much to the delight of the old man. The estate was eventually split between our care and the neighbor who had probably earned it very well.

3) The over-worked decision. This is a decision made many times—before and after the action decided upon has been accomplished. We have seen residents move to our center and rehash the decision repeatedly. Years after having presumably settled the matter, they conduct a debate with themselves and with the few who will listen. It is a little like the gentleman who celebrated his fiftieth wedding anniversary wondering if he had married the right woman. He never let the decision rest.

4) The split decision. This form of decision-making meets competing needs. The individual avoids insecurity by not leaving his or her home, knowing it is impossible to remain there. So he or she fills out the application, pays a deposit on an apartment, visits the facility repeatedly, talks to friends, but never does leave home. The paperwork appeases the family, who are sure he or she must do something. But never moving lets the person remain attached to a treasured abode. Each time a relative implores that individual to move to a place where he or she will be cared for, another visit is paid and another report duly made to the irritated relative. Thus the person quiets his or her relative and satisfies self, at least until the matter comes up again.

5) Realistic decider. These folks have accurately assessed their needs, looked over alternatives, discussed issues with their families, come to a conclusion, and acted. They are happy in their move and express little regret, though they miss elements of their previous situation. But they define their move in positive terms and regard it as a step forward. These people make the best adjustments and become happy residents. When the need for long confinement comes, as it sometimes does, they also see that as the best alternative available and are thankful for having a facility available.

These types of decisions are not unique to older people. If you look carefully, you can probably find yourself in one of the categories, even if you are only 30 years old. The quality of our decision making is based upon vitality of our spiritual and mental health. Strong people make positive decisions, even if they cause some trouble. Weaker souls whine a bit and make less than satisfactory moves, which in turn set up circumstances for more unfortunate results. But the cycle can be broken, and by making good rational moves we ready ourselves for maximum possibilities.

References

1. Ahlem, Lloyd H. Quality of Life in Covenant Retirement Communities (Unpublished research, 1985).
2. O'Connor, Nancy, Letting Go With Love (Tuscon: La Mariposa Press, 1984), pp. 158-161.

Questions for Discussion

1. Reflect on the stress factors and uplifts mentioned at the beginning of this chapter. Does your experience verify these items. How is your experience different? Would you add or subtract any items in the two lists?
2. Several types of responses to change are mentioned. Which of these most fits your experience? Or do you vary in typc of rc-sponse depending on the problem being solved? If so, how do you vary?
3. Do you ever find yourself in conflict with someone close to you who responds very differently to change?

SIX

Aging in the Family System

Martha is 80 years old, single, and living with her brother and his family. She retired 15 years ago, and serves as a housekeeper to help her brother and his wife hold full-time jobs. Martha's brother is 20 years younger and a few years away from retirement. The couple have teenage children, still attending school—the fruits of a late marriage.

Martha and her brother lost their parents when they were quite young. Martha assumed a single parent's role, providing for her brother by working as a bookkeeper. When he graduated from high school, he became a machinist's apprentice and together they bought a modest home. Twenty years later they retired the mortgage. Through years of inflation, the twenty-thousand-dollar home became a two-hundred-thousand-dollar asset.

But then her brother met an attractive woman, ten years his junior. Romance flourished and the couple married. The new bride moved in with her husband and Martha, and with minor adjustments, life went reasonably well. When the couple became parents of two daughters and a son, the three-bedroom home bulged to house a four-bedroom family. Nerves frayed as the growing kids played their stereos, brought in boisterous friends, and challenged Martha's cherished domestic authority. Three children of both sexes occupying a single bedroom isn't the best during adolescence, either. So they divided it into very small cubicles, making solitude very rare. The youngest daughter stays away evenings, spending far less time than she should at home. Home is but a parking lot and filling station. She rushes in, dashes out, avoiding contact as much as possible. Rumors persist she is running with a loose crowd. When she slows down enough to talk, she usually threatens to move out, a giant step for a 13 year old.

Martha increasingly resents her brother's kids. But they see her as an interfering old lady and openly gripe about her. Martha responds that this is her home, too. Furthermore, she cannot afford to leave, especially at her age. Neither can her brother afford to buy her out. Age and economics have trapped them together. Caught between warring parties, the brother tries to solve the problem by cautioning his children to stop irritating their aunt and mind their own business. The children's mother stays uninvolved directly, but as the war has heated up, she has become ill with debilitating stomach problems.

The mother is unable to work and has taken an extended leave. But at home all the time, Martha lectures her about laxness in making the kids mind. It's a topic she won't leave alone and gets around to at least once a day—with fervor. Soon the leave will end and the mother must return to work, resign, or be terminated. Family income is down because the mother is not working. Father's cautions are useless. Mother shows no improvement, and Martha is grinding out endless moralisms about the kids upbringing. Tough questions press upon the family. Who is at fault? Who makes a move to ease the tension? How long can we endure without doing something? Martha's solution is that the kids must shut up and mind! Father's solution is to avoid conflict—withdraw. The kids solution is for Martha to die and make another bedroom available. They hope the family will inherit her money, too!

Interestingly, the children have been helpful to their mother by turning down their stereos. The youngest is spending less time away from home. But the kids have turned up the stress on Martha and often are in open conflict with her. Thus we have an aging person in a system of tensions that has precipitated illness and conflict. But Mother's solution is to get sick. That forces attention upon her and away from the conflict. But it also reduces income and tightens the budget. What if her husband loses his job? If she gets well, attention returns to the conflict with Martha. Then what? Martha and family provide an example of how people work and live in tension systems. Conflicting individuals play one against the other, balancing tension in various ways. Or they can gang up on one person and make that one the victim, thus reducing the tension for the rest of them. This is the balance struck in this family so far.

Two books in recent years have helped our understanding of how family systems work—Virginia Satir's *Conjoint Family Therapy*[1] and

Edwin Friedman's *From Generation to Generation.*[2] Satir suggests that our problems have much to do with our relational networks and how we stand in them and respond to their forces. Individual problems may be less important in explaining behavior than the system in which they occur. Friedman further develops applications to church congregations and demonstrates intergenerational explanations for behavior.

Following are a number of principles in systems behavior:

1) When systems become stressed, symptoms are likely to emerge in one member. This member may be an unwitting volunteer to bear the symptoms, or be conscripted for the purpose of symptom-bearing. In the illustration of Martha and clan, the mother was an unwitting volunteer. During counseling, she reasoned that if she had not married and had not brought children into the system there would have been no trouble. Therefore, she was to blame. By "volunteering" to be ill she absorbed the stress of the situation and "atoned" for her fault. She became what systems psychologists call the identified symptom bearer, or ISB. Note that the youngest girl, who was staying away too much, ceased her most difficult behavior when mother became ill. The child and her mother traded places. At first the child was the identified symptom bearer, then the mother. But not wanting to add to her mother's stress, the daughter alleviated it by behaving better. The system could now be balanced without her misbehavior. If mother becomes well again, we might wonder who will "volunteer" to be the next ISB.

2) Considering family problems as systems problems avoids isolating one individual for all the attention. If the misbehaving daughter had remained the ISB, and mother not volunteered to be ill, the family could have focused on the daughter by agreeing that she was the problem and sought assistance for her. She might well have seen a counselor and been given insights to help her understand that she was not improving matters by running with her questionable friends and staying away so much. But her behavior probably would not have changed much. By becoming "normal," the stress would have to be shifted. The family system would be unbalanced again. If it was agreed that she was the problem the family might resist the child's returning to normal, for they would no longer have a person on whom to project the stress and blame. Until the whole family understood that all were involved in sharing the stress and in the balancing act, the ultimate solution would not be

found. Instead they would continue refocusing until someone became the permanent ISB.

3) Every system seeks balance. In the case cited, balance was attempted through the mother's illness. That illness focused attention away from conflict with Martha and got the misbehaving daughter to do better. But it might have been balanced by making the younger child ill. Or it might have heaped stress on Martha, possibly precipitating her death. In unhealthy systems, or in dysfunctional families, insecure members put others down. Weaker members accept these putdowns and with damaged self-images either become ill or develop into trouble-makers. Dysfunctional systems need a victim! Martha refused to be the victim and the youngest daughter became the ISB until mother volunteered. People learn to play one off the other to balance systems under tension.

Business groups and families will tolerate trouble-makers to endless lengths because they balance the system by providing a victim. The same systems will reject creative thinkers and free spirits because they unbalance the system! Such people generate too many ideas to assimilate, or they juggle power structures. Innovation is psychologically risky, often more threatening than illness. Thus it is possible for families, businesses organizations, and churches to stay ill longer than the lifetime of any of their members. One generation passes on to the next the stresses and balancing methods of the previous one. When the ISB of one generation passes away or moves out, new ones are recruited to fill the part.

Suppose Martha was not so stubborn about the children's behavior. Or suppose that Martha was a "shrinking violet" personality, or that she was not half-owner of the house. Would she more likely have become the ISB in the family? Perhaps so, and perhaps the reasons are shared by older people in general. Consider the following:

a) Older people, especially the very old, require more attention than younger and therefore are more vulnerable to becoming the focus of stress in families. Once focused upon for their weaknesses, they become targets for other stresses the system may need to resolve. It is easier to select an older person to be the ISB than a younger one because of the natural weaknesses of age.

b) Older people are perceived as having less to lose than younger people and can be selected easily as victims. In Martha's case, the family might force her out of the system by placing her in a care facility. This is not an uncommon solution and is easily justified by its perpetrators. Martha has only a short life expectancy, so not much is lost by removing her.

c) Older people are regarded as less educated than the younger and may be perceived as lacking knowledge common to high-tech times. Seen as naive, they are more easily dismissed as insignificant contributors in the system's decision-making. It is easier, in the name of superior knowledge, to impose decisions upon older people they may not desire for themselves.

I keep a watchful eye out for employees who use position and expertise as reasons for shuffling residents and patients into places that make them easier to manage. I recall a "straw-boss" type of nurse whose reason for moving residents into health care units was her inability to keep them from bothering her too much. When they asserted their needs, rather than their docility, she relocated them. Their increasing need was not going to add to her work load. Reducing freedom of choice and independence was her way of managing. She looked good on efficiency ratings, but the psychological costs were devastating. I wonder how Martha, with her tendency to carp about problems, would have been treated if she were weak and subjected to the system controlled by this "straw boss." Unfortunately, older people deprived of freedom of choice and independence become ill more quickly. The "straw boss" approach is clearly counter-productive.

4) When forced to become an ISB, victims learn to become manipulative, using illness as a weapon. My father had a friend he described as "enjoying ill health until the day he died." He was talented, but a loner. Overprotected as a youth, he made few friends. To gain attention, he developed allergies and stomach problems. He traveled continuously in his work, sending menus ahead to hotels and homes where he was to stay. He never felt secure without extra service, a need generated in his developing years. Every retirement center administrator knows well a resident who manipulates with illness. It is a handy means of securing favors, bargaining for treats, or getting transportation. It can be used to relocate family gatherings, reallocate financial resources, deny access to relationships, or avoid confrontations. Illness is surrendered reluctantly if it serves as an effective lever.

5) Systems last longer than people; they extend through several generations. Systems and the means of manipulation are taught to

heirs. I know of one church more than 100 years old that cannot change pastors without going through convulsions. Each generation teaches the next one clumsy methods of change. One pastor left to assume a prestigious university post and the congregation was at a loss because it had not had its usual blood-letting. Furthermore, it is possible to rule systems from the grave, controlling family fortunes and properties. One gentleman started a business that made him wealthy. He brought his five children into the business to be sure they would be well provided for. Some had little talent for the work, but his needs for their security were intense. So they reluctantly stayed with it. About to die in his early sixties, he gathered his offspring and secured a promise from each that they would never give up the business until the last one was left to make a sale. As you might guess, the children have had war to wage. Business needs singular authority, and five people can't decide who is boss. The oldest one assumed the manager role, but with little interest or aptitude for the work. Business is slowly declining and will likely die before any of them. Two of the heirs see the folly of their death-bed promise and want to sell out. But two others are so laden with guilt they cannot agree to the sale.

We learn to get old by watching our parents. We repeat what the previous generation has taught us unless we consciously change our behavior. We can do this readily, if we so resolve, but we may reject change because of the value of the manipulative behaviors we have learned. As we get older and decline in assumed hierarchical powers, we are increasingly tempted to be manipulative. If the system we live in is unhealthy, lurching and grinding and making people ill, to yield power is to accept grave danger. There is an inverse relation between our psychological health and our tendency to be manipulative. People with unresolved problems constantly seek to control and maneuver others. But manipulation has a no-win result. Manipulation soon becomes harmful to relationships and only teaches the same to one's heirs. On the other hand, emotionally healthy older people have the ability to accept their losses and preserve their relationships—a great lesson to teach the next generation.

6) Our systems fail when they are inflexible or ineffectual. Aging creates the need for flexibility. Losses in aging change the systems we live in. We must give power over matters to someone at some point. We cannot vigorously pursue our vocations or manage our affairs forever. We are increasingly dependent, whether we want to

be or not. In healthy systems, power surrender is relief. But if we are beset with insecurity that will not allow for normal change, surrender is grief.

I worked with a young girl who haggled constantly with her mother. She was insolent and rude, refusing to go to church or make any commitments to faith—a supreme insult to her parents. Mother was domineering and demanded "fixing" for her daughter's spiritual rebellion. As the girl and I talked, anger permeated her words. She obviously was not going to be "fixed"! Mother was recruiting her to bear the stress of the family and she would have none of it. No psychologist was going to help mother victimize her! Our interviews ended shortly. Years later I discovered that the mother had had a stroke and was totally dependent upon her. The daughter had taken over Mother's dress shop as well as her care. She took Mother to work each day in a wheel chair—drooling into her clothes, and taking verbal abuse when no customers were around. An inflexible system had failed the daughter, and now retaliation was being reaped against the mother. Strangely, the daughter appeared serene, in control, satisfied that she could get even. But I wondered how her conscience would fare if retaliation continued for long. I also wondered what the daughter would do if her children repeated the drama for her when she was old.

7) Systems that succeed have several characteristics.

a) They establish good feedback systems so people can hear each other and modify their behavior appropriately. Members tell accurate stories to each other and communicate honest feelings. Very little "decoding" of either words or behavior is necessary. This keeps the information trustworthy so people can make good adjustments to each other and not compound their agonies. Times for talking are plentiful. No one gets "loaded up" without an opportunity to vent his or her feelings.

b) Members allow for normal growth and change to take place. I know an old couple who still talk to their adult children as if they were third graders, giving advice on every minor detail of their lives. I also know adult children who refuse to recognize that their parents are old and depend needlessly upon them, creating expectations older people can't handle. Older people need to be able to reduce their power without loss of integrity. Seniors need as much control over their own decisions as possible, perhaps fumbling first but then yielding to those who can assist. Members must be able to feed back their changing needs so systems won't get stuck. We are not third graders forever; and neither are we young and healthy forever.

c) When healthy systems work, they focus more on members most capable of effecting change. An identified symptom-bearer may have the most problems visible, but how can someone loaded with stress change the milieu he or she is swimming in? Such a person will surely need support, but there is likely little energy or insight to make the system better that weighs that person down. Think of Martha again. Does she have the greatest capacity to effect change—to balance the system? If she voluntarily agreed to leave the home and enter other quarters would that allow Mother to become well again? Would it be Father if he realized his aloofness was leaving others to flounder? Could Martha learn that her carping about the children's behavior was counter-productive and making Mother ill?

Typical counseling practice would select the symptom-bearer for help and focus therapy on that person. It is no wonder such counsel is unproductive. Up tight and tense, such a one often has little capacity for effecting change. If counsel persuaded the symptom-bearer to drop the symptoms, that person might be crushed. Symptoms are protective shields the mind erects to protect from further hurt. When symptoms are surrendered , the hurting person is exposed to renewed psychological danger. We are not psychological islands, solving problems without consideration of the milieu in which problems are found. With older people, as with Martha, the entire system—or family in this case—must adjust together. It will be of little use to counsel only Martha, or only the father or daughter. All will need to work to create peace and balance the system.

d) Healthy systems charge minimal emotional prices for failure and readily extend help for rescue. One of the ways people abuse power in systems is to charge a "shame tax" when someone fails. Satirical or abusive comments, denial of privilege or freedom, or exacting confessions are all part of soliciting the shame tax. Healthy members have learned to refuse shame tax payments and make adjustments without being put upon by manipulative members. Thus rescue in a healthy system is much easier than in a sick system, for the integrity of each member is fully respected.

e) Successful systems allow members to define personal goals apart from group pressures. This is especially important for older people. Often adult children will push parents to come to decisions about themselves. But all people need emotional "wiggle room" to test an idea, to try out a solution, or adapt to a new situation. Seniors need as much responsibility for their destinies as they can manage, but they need room to wiggle their way to good decisions. Imposing solutions or rushing to conclusions is coercive and muddles both thought and feeling.

f) Healthy systems avoid "stuck togetherness." Some families appear to be extremely close. But one soon learns that unusual closeness can be unhealthy. In such systems freedom for great change is forbidden. Neither can a solicitous favor be rejected. You must accept the favor and allow it to become a debt you must pay later. You must not rock the boat. You must always be ready to explain your behavior. Healthy systems, on the other hand, let people come and go, approach and withdraw, while working out solutions to problems or making major life changes.

g) Healthy systems develop members who become integrated, whole people. They are not fiercely independent and they are not helplessly dependent. They can turn to the system for support and can turn aside for help the system cannot provide. Every system should be a supply of grace for its members. But it should not play God. All of us as aging persons are capable of more than we have traditionally thought possible if we maintain healthy relationships. In healthy systems we can also yield ourselves up when we must without a fuss. Hopefully we will also be remembered as people without a need to rule from the grave.

References

1. Satir, Virginia, *Conjoint Family Therapy*, 3rd ed. (Palo Alto California: Science and Behavior Books, 1983).
2. Friedman, Edwin H., *From Generation to Generation: Family Process in Church and Synagogue* (New York: The Guilford Press, 1985).

Questions For Discussion

1. Review your family system. Can you name any ISBs?
2. Who manifested most power in your family? How was it used? Who manifested least? How did that person behave?
3. How did you find your place in the system? Describe your role. Describe how you maneuvered to change and adapt to the system.
4. List the attributes of health in the system in which you live. What liabilities seem to be there?

5. What was the most satisfying part of living in your family system? What bothered you most?
6. What have you done to make your place and method of change more healthy and satisfying in your system? When things don't go well, from whom do you seek help?
7. Who is the oldest person in your family system? What role is played by that person? How does that person effect the system?
8. What special problems are there for the older members of your system?

SEVEN

Effects of Age on Relationships

A good friend, 17 years my senior, and I were playing a tough university golf course one fall when we joined a twosome, both younger and both good golfers. My friend had been a professional athlete and his game reflected his natural ability. My game was in good shape, too, and I was thoroughly enjoying shooting "over my head" this beautiful morning. The twosome soon took note of our crisp shots and precise putts and expressed wonderment that two old-looking duffers could play so well. My grubby beard and old clothes probably helped me look more years than I had lived. We finished the round with compliments from the younger two, generously overstated. Then one of them turned to me and said, "You must have been some kind of golfer in your young days!" My older partner laughed so loud he was embarrassed, but promptly retorted, "This kid is all of 59 years old! What do you mean—in his younger days? He's just getting started!"

Our story illustrates that with age we get certain deferences we had not known previously. If we played again and put a little money on the game, the deferences likely would have disappeared. Age gets us deference without granting us advantage. In fact, deference is often a sop for denying equality. The employment market is example enough. In our dotage, we are treated kindly until we prove ourselves a threat. Older people find themselves accepted until they prove they can fully join the competitive fray; then they are often victims of discrimination. In other words age brings us kindness and deference, but with exclusions and discriminations. We may benefit from the force of law in protecting our rights, but equality is still an uphill climb.

My daughter and son-in-law, with our grandchild in arms, came to visit us one weekend—only to find that we had gone to a party. The gala was long and late, but unusually full of fun. We lingered until the wee hours and would have continued longer if we could have kept our eyes open. When we returned home, our daughter and husband were up waiting for us, deeply concerned that we might have gotten into trouble. "Honey!" my wife announced, "Now you know how we felt sitting up for you when you were out partying. It's nice of you to be concerned, but I don't think we're ready for role reversal yet. Go to bed and stop worrying. We can still take care of ourselves."

Age does change roles, but this reversal was a bit premature. When age reduces our capacities some productive shifting of responsibilities may be in order but the shifts have to be done carefully. It is no use to expect older parents to make someone else responsible for their feelings, values, or attitudes. These mind-sets will always be theirs. Conflicts erupt quickly when younger people assume they must change older people's views and feelings. On the other hand, it is entirely possible and often proper for management of property, other tasks, and legal responsibilities to be shifted to children.

Parents easily feel responsible for their adult children's well being, but brothers and sisters may care and counsel when their siblings are in need. I recall one of our sons having a particular problem at work, one that he would usually have discussed with me. When I found that his brother-in-law had much better counsel, I was relieved, finding my role had changed and I would not need to be as deeply involved as I had once been. The more I thought about it, the more thankful I became. But I also have friends who feel rejected when their children talk more among themselves and less to them about major concerns. Age may retire us from caregiver to observer and if our egos are touchy it will hurt. But the change is unburdening and we ought to enjoy the relief! Maybe the change will be as dramatic as one expressed on a bumper sticker I saw recently: "Avenge Yourself! Live Long Enough to Be a Problem to Your Children!" Role reversal is normal but not for every aspect of living.

This leads to a third important effect that age brings to relationships. The dependency of older people is a significant achievement or failure opportunity for their children. Recently, a couple came to one of our centers and inquired about costs of entering. As we talked, they were very dismayed for they had limited resources. They apologized for having taken my time and said they would discuss their problem with their son who had sent them to inquire. I thought I would not see them again. Two days later the son stopped by and asked how our interview had gone. I remembered their disappointment and told him I saw little chance of them getting in. Then the son broke into a big smile and said, "I have never really known what my folks resources were, so I sent them here partly to have them fill out the financial declaration so I could find out. Now if you will tell me what they need, I will pay any difference so they can come to live in this fine facility." I phoned the parents who readily agreed to reveal their needs to their son. They were delighted that he cared so much, even though their fierce independence had to give way a bit. "Please tell our son we do not want to be a burden to him. This is too much!" "I don't think it is too much for him," I replied. "He sees this as a great opportunity to thank you for being fine parents. He's going to get more satisfaction out of this than you are." The parents have since passed away, but whenever I see the son he still smiles with satisfaction that he was able to give an assist to well-deserving, loving parents. He never regarded it as an expense; it was a gift he very much desired to give. He counts it as one of his life's most significant achievements.

On the other hand, I have seen miserly children, blessed with assets but burdened with selfishness, who would not risk a nickel for needy parents. When eventual trouble came, they were grief-stricken because their unwillingness magnified problems that could have been easily solved with modest expenditures. Parents can resist assistance too much and deprive both themselves and offspring of a valuable experience. Children thrive on opportunities to help—to evidence maturity of relationship to money and a venture into selflessness.

Parents and children become peers in important areas of life. My son lost his best friend to a drunk's inability to control his automobile. We shared the grief, not as a parent consoling a child but as adults feeling the same loss. Similarly, my daughter is a confidante to a friend who has a drinking problem. Together we share a prayer agenda to lend support in the struggle. Another son was stimulated to deeper understanding of the New Testament parables by a very effective teacher in college. As we discussed the stories, I realized that we were equals seeking deeper understanding of the truths involved. His more recent study gave me insights I did not have before; my experience added depth to his knowledge. We were peers growing side by side.

My oldest son and I play in golf tournaments together from time to time. We are teammates on nearly equal footing and have a few trophies to show for it. I can't stay with him in basketball or softball—I'm too slow and stiff. But we are equals in many things, and the father/son differences have diminished to near equality. Some of my children have larger paychecks than I have. We talk together about financial plans, investments, advancements in jobs—not as parents telling kids what to do, but as equals sharing counsel about the future. We once gave advice on how to feel about such matters, but we don't do that often any more. Dictated attitudes never take root; they only create resentment that spoils relationships. By the time our children are mid-teenagers, our capacity to determine their attitudes about anything is minimal. In matters of attitude, values, feelings, we are equals. Neither generation can impose feelings on the other. Only encouragement and care can nudge change in these matters.

Age is an opportunity for a second exchange of primary affectional relationships. When I was a school psychologist I counseled with a 40-year-old woman who had gone into serious though temporary depression. At first she talked of her symptoms, her lack of understanding why she felt so badly, and finally her grief. Her 16-year-old son had fallen madly in love for the first time and was totally focused on his relationship with his girl friend. It was a normal, wholesome teenage romance. But Mother could hardly stand to hear the girl's name—a name uttered every moment when the boy was home. The woman's husband had died two years previously, and the son was her great source of consolaton and affection. One evening as she drove up to her home, she spotted the two hugging in the living room while watching TV. Mother confessed that she felt like a jilted wife, a discarded lover, a replaced confidante, an unneeded friend. Shocked at her own reactions, she had not realized how much she depended on her son. She knew such a moment would arrive, but she did not comprehend how deeply she would feel about it. Her son had exchanged her for another as the object of his primary affections.

I recall a story about a father who had given his daughter in marriage to his new son-in-law and now sat glumly at the table for the couple's wedding reception. The pastor who had performed the ceremony turned to him and said, "Jake, you look like you had just lost your most important friend!" "More than that," replied Jake. "I feel like I just gave away my Stradivarius to a gorilla!" Primary affections moved from Dad to lover and Dad hurt!

One of the beautiful experiences in aging surrounds youngsters returning to the primary affectional relationship we once enjoyed with them. As adults in well-formed marriages, our kids are secure enough to be "mushy" again. And we love it! Once we were traded off for peers we scarcely knew; now we rejoin the affectionate circle again. Not that our children have traded off their mates for us; they have merely found it possible to share their affections with us again. When my sons were late teenagers there was no way I could give them a hug and a kiss. But now that they are in their late thirties, we can hug and tease with that old cuddly stuff again. Maturity and emotional growth makes it all possible, one the great blessings of being older. For those who are having trouble managing these changes, here are a few tips for you.

1) Take time. Don't force or crowd feelings in any relationship. Let each one have as much emotional wiggle room as possible. Normal, healthy feelings are desired by those concerned and they will gravitate toward these feelings if not under a great deal of pressure.

2) Listen a lot. Watch the talk ratio. Those who feel they must talk most of the time will turn off those they want to get close to.

3) Listen more carefully to the feelings being expressed than to the ideas stated. It is possible to answer every question raised and miss the point if feelings are ignored. Listen especially to the matters that seem most stress-laden. That is at the heart of the concern—don't miss it!

4) Don't reject or correct feelings. Feelings are not subject to easy, voluntary control. People feel personally rejected when their feelings are slighted. Assure the person you are talking with that you hear how they are feeling.

5) Ask lots of open-ended questions. Avoid the things that can be answered true or false—or with a this or that, a yes or no. Feelings are neither true nor false but mixtures of both and need many expressions to be understood.

6) Review your style and the manner of meeting changes you encountered in the past. Were your methods effective? Did you put people off? Do you have a high or low casualty rate in former relationships? Some changes in style may be in order.

7) Arrange for several situations in which relationships can correct themselves and grow. Set up events that are going to be very

low-stress experiences and remove the troublesome aspects of the relationship from these events. Trust can be built in these situations that will carry over to more direct meetings concerning problems that have arisen.

8) Kindly caring is the best technique in mending problems. It isn't necessary to be psychologically astute or have a "gee whiz" personality to be caring and kindly. Kindness with persistence will overcome nearly any barrier between people.

Questions for Discussion.

1. Has anyone tried to take over a bit of your life and run it for you? How does that feel? What did you do to guard against such intrusions? What advice do you have for others who experienced the same?
2. Has someone you have been close to recently tried to change your feeling about yourself or your values? How did you respond? What emotions did you sense?
3. Would you describe yourself as fiercely independent or heavily dependent? Or somewhere in between? In what matters are you most likely to be either dependent or independent?
4. Is it difficult for you to accept gifts of help or assistance in later years? Has anyone expressed feelings of being put off by your response to their overtures? What would it cost you emotionally to become either more dependent or more independent? Are you headed in either direction, viewing your reactions of recent years?
5. Share an experience that has been especially rewarding to you as a peer to your children. Did the children feel as you do about the experience?
6. What do your children accomplish that truly makes you a believer in heredity?

EIGHT

Conflicts in Aging

Millie was a kindergarten teacher who met a large group of howlers when school started one fall. After a couple of days of tear-drying and shooing anxious mothers out of her classroom, she flopped into a chair in the teachers lounge and moaned, "If I could skip the first week of school and start with the second this would be a great job! But domesticating these little rug rats is getting worse every year." These are tense times for five year olds as they break into a big new world. Millie was the emotional midwife during a great transition in the lives of young children.

I think of a friend just back from his honeymoon. The couple had been to a national park for two weeks, been rained on every day, shooed away bears, slept on hard ground, and ate scores of baking powder biscuits cooked over a fire neither of them knew how to start. They finally came home, crabbing at each other because it was the worst trip either had ever taken. The bliss of romance was lost in mud, body odor, bad food, and testy personalities.

In transition, uncertainties stimulate stress and conflict. The kindergarten kids crabbed and fought. The honeymooners griped and argued. It's not so different from changes in aging. Ending a career, entering a retirement facility, losing a spouse, major illnesses, repositioning finances—all can upset us and make us feisty. Transitions alter power and relationships in our family systems and we must adjust accordingly. I knew a woman who could not manage her finances very well and turned over her checkbook to her daughter. It was a very helpful move, because overdraft statements stopped coming, bills got paid, and checks were cashed. Both the mother and daughter breathed easier in the peace it brought. But Mother was declining in health and the daughter decided to move her to a care facility. The daughter assumed the move was obviously needed and her mother would easily concur. But Mother would have none of it. The fight was on! To forestall the change, she called a taxi, went to the bank, revoked the daughter's power of attorney for her accounts, and canceled her deposit at the care center. This move returned power to the mother in relationship to her family, but it renewed the financial chaos that had been resolved. After more disasters with unpaid bills, Mother gathered all her deposit slips, overdraft notices, uncashed checks, and a sack full of miscellaneous receipts and dumped them in her daughter's lap. But the surrender of financial power reopened the argument about moving to a care center. Having lost the power of money, Mother needed another lever to preserve her control. Conflict was her choice and a full-blown storm ensued.

While starting a fight can be one way of preventing decisions and perhaps restoring power, it often creates more problems than it solves. Tensions rise, relationships are broken, family members cease discussions, and power gravitates to one dominant personality. The problem might have been solved by a healthy discussion, but the daughter saw herself as being in charge—money-power implies authority—and produced a solution. Mother saw herself as a loser in the family system and started fights to save her control. Both could have done a little psychological cost-accounting before they acted. Mother needed time to realize her increasing dependency and the daughter needed to know the emotional price of abrupt change for her parent. Mark it firmly that in great changes psychological costs are usually heavier than the financial burdens borne. People need plenty of wiggle room to manage tough transitions. Adult children who pride themselves on efficiency and prompt problem solving can wreak havoc on the feelings of their parents. If older people have limited insight or are inflexible in attitude, larger, more intense conflicts occur. Such minds feel much more is at stake since they visualize fewer alternatives for themselves. Furthermore, age amplifies personality quirks and makes them sharpen the conflict.

Several types of conflicts have been noted by writers in this field. In *Aging Parent,*[1] edited by Pauline Ragan, three types of conflicts are identified:

1) Sustained conflicts. These are arguments about personal lifestyles, behavior and morals, religious commitment and values, and social attitudes. These conflicts were likely to have developed in childhood and continued ever since. If the child has moved away,

the conflict is not aroused and stays subdued until the parent rejoins the adult child's family system. Since rejoining usually occurs on the adult child's ground rather than the parent's turf, the parent is less able to lever the argument to his or her favor. Stress is amplified.

2) Recycled conflicts. These conflicts, sometimes called reactivated conflicts, usually are unresolved battles for control. They were unfinished when the child left the parental family system and haven't bothered anybody much since. But when the parent rejoins the system, now controlled by the adult child, battles resume.

I use the term "recycled" because the battle most often has changed its character. Since years have passed between the child's exit and the parent's return, tactics have changed and adult children are more sophisticated battlers than when they were young. They have sharpened their weapons and become more adept in their use. They have also become more subtle and are not given so much to direct attack. Friends or siblings may carry part of the thrust. But the parent likely battles as if the children were still kids.

Two elements in recycled conflicts are important. First, conflict probably will be played out at a different point of contact between contending parties. I remember a son who faithfully called on his mother in a nursing home. They had a long history of warring over the son's choice of friends and activities. Now the son avoided discussion of that old problem by walking away when it came up. So mother created another bothersome problem for them to deal with. On each visit she would insist on having some troublesome task done for her, timing her request about the time the son wanted to leave. The chore was symbolic of her need to have her will carried out in his life, even if she was denied the privilege of carping about her son's friends. He dutifully carried out the chore, finding the game humorous—knowing her days of real control were long gone and had only a nuisance effect now.

The second important element in recycled conflicts is that they become internalized. An internalized conflict occurs when one person has taken both sides of the battle into him- or herself. Thus the war goes on in his or her mind, much like a battle of conscience. For example, Lucy is a fastidious housekeeper and hates the fact. Her hate is a hangover from younger days when her mother made her scrub, scour, and disinfect every inch of the house. Saturdays were dreaded because she and her mother crusaded against germs until she was bone tired. Furthermore she had no time for fun with friends and often cried as she watched them play. When she cleans her house now, she can still hear her mother's admonitions that cleanliness is a moral issue. And if she isn't fastidious, she feels guilty, years after leaving home. Her mother has been dead for a long while but the conflict continues, all within Lucy's head. One day Lucy's husband remarked that the floor in the shower was getting a little gray, and Lucy blew her stack. Poor husband did not know that he had set off a bomb. For a few minutes Lucy hated him with all the passion she used to hate Saturdays.

In times of great change, old conflicts will muddle current decisions. It takes some grace and maturity not to deal with an old fight as a present contention. A little time out, backing away, and rethinking what is happening will reduce present tensions helpfully. Problems can last beyond the lifetime of conflicting parties. I have known adult children visiting graves of their parents to conduct an argument, with nobody available to talk back. Likewise, I have known couples who divorce, but one has internalized the problem and continues the strife long after the spouses have separated. Thus conflict is continued, and dumped on the next generation, a new spouse, or anyone close to the situation. Friends of mine have distant relatives in Europe who kept a family feud going for at least five generations. Had no one internalized the dispute and dumped it on the next generation, it could have been resolved a hundred years ago.

3) New conflicts. New conflicts are those that arise when a parent rejoins the family. These conflicts have no long-standing antecedents, but arise out of new circumstances amplified by problems of aging. While older persons are not disengaging from life, they are reducing the number of points of contact with life and emphasizing the psychological value of the points selected. For example, husbands and wives spend more time together in old age than previously, with more personal value invested in their relationship. If one of the partners passes away, the surviving spouse may turn in dependency or attachment to an adult child, creating demands for time and attention that can't be mustered. Conflict arises and the parent may complain that important needs are being ignored or personal interests aren't worth attention. Or a dominant wife loses a dependent husband and tries to dominate her son-in-law instead. In this case we see recycling taking place, as well as new conflict arising. It is recycling because this is the habitual pattern for the

parent but a new conflict for the son-in-law. New conflicts will tend to focus upon high-stress events that occur in old age: repositioning of assets, health care, chronic illnesses, too much property to manage, or changing standards of behavior. As these normal events occur, we need to remember that transitions are in effect and neutral zones of these transitions are the most vulnerable to conflict. Conflict may become a tool to shorten time and express uncertainty in the neutral zone. Conflicts will be precipitated to get matters settled. But if settling by means of conflict is premature, outcomes are complicated. Then settlements reached must be undone and new ones constructed, doubling stresses experienced. But if conflict gets results for an older person, it may become addictive. Addiction then becomes a separate and complicated problem in an already messy relational environment.

In *Living With Stress,*[2] I outlined the traditional method of conflict resolution. Here are the key ideas. These will help most in new conflicts, though possibly in old or recycled conflicts as well.

1) First, identify the problem and the possible gains and losses for the parties involved, including psychological losses. This may take time and effort because most of us do not know what our losses will cost emotionally.

2) Recognize that some of our problems may be symbolic of conflicts in other areas of life. Recycled conflicts often become symbolic. If we discover we are using one arena of life to solve a problem combatively in another, that is not a reason to demean anyone so doing.

3) Abandon the "I must win" motive. This is the largest hurdle in reaching a solution. Surrender feels emotionally costly. If our egos are tender, it takes much effort to relinquish the motive to win. But little can be achieved unless surrender occurs.

4) Work at several possible solutions. Then place the alternatives in order of mutual preference. If the first one fails, move to the second. If only one solution is generated, the party most effected may see him- or herself the loser without recourse. We all need exits occasionally from solutions, with opportunity to try new ones.

5) Evaluate the results. Agree to conduct a review ahead of time. Since solutions cost someone power, prestige, or ego, costs may be greater or less than expected. It may be necessary to balance costs so no one finds the price of solution too high. In successful solutions, no one feels completely like a loser and a good relationship can be

built for future discussion.

Having stated methods of resolution, know also that there are several types of conflict participants. Combatants learn several styles. You might find yourself in the following list:

1) Conflict addicts. The method of conflict resolution just stated will not apply when you encounter the addicts. They need conflict. Their adrenaline rushes and gives them a “high” when they are fighting. They are like the fire engine chaser, except that they chase stress. If their environment isn’t charging them up, they start a fight. They feel more secure when others are thrown off balance in conflict.

I had an employee once who couldn’t stand continual peace. If things were too calm, he would start stirring. “Did you hear about...? What are you going to do about it?” he would gossip. If we had reached a solution to a problem, he would soon want to review it and change it. He felt exposed, psychologically, by tranquility. Basically an anxious person, he was not comfortable until everyone else was stewing over something. Whatever the supposed problem, it was always presented logically—never as a product of his stirrings. If I did not jump to solve his problem he would get an ally to get things moving. Until I confronted him and gave an ultimatum to stop, we had little peace. Even then we had to think twice before reacting to his concerns very much. Part of the only solution was to avoid giving that employee a platform on which to amplify his grievances. This included coffee breaks and department meetings. We put him last on the agenda in department meetings and ignored his gossip at break time.

Addicts need attention. But if you deprive them of their stirrings, they must be attended to in other ways. If they do not get your eye, they circle around and make themselves felt elsewhere. Plan on a portion of your time for them, because they are going to get it one way or another. But limit it closely to help them get attention in useful ways without becoming an emotional drain-time for many.

2) Solution asserters. These are the folks that have a solution before they know what the problem is. They feel uncomfortable unless they are fixing something all the time. They are put off by long examinations of alternatives. They dislike solutions proposed by people they do not value.

I served on a corporate trustee board once with a man of just such a nature. We were struggling miserably with a problem on which opinion was strongly divided. Weary of discussion after ten minutes he blurted, "Let's get everybody together in one place and have it out once and for all!" Such a proposal would have only expanded the arena for controversy and settled nothing. But he couldn't wait. Such participants need help to see the lack of productivity in their efforts. Their anxiety overflows beyond its proportional right and they are adding—not subtracting—stress. The resolution method, listed earlier and rigidly adhered to, will be a good education for such a combatant. Usually he or she is driven by poor self-image and must have peace, even if it means dealing with his or her own feelings before dealing with the problem correctly.

3) Ostriches. These actively avoid conflict. Peace at any price is their motive. They avoid recycled conflict especially. To experience conflict is to feel guilty. Such a person has probably fared badly in conflict and been blamed for bad outcomes of conflict. He or she needs encouragement, prodding, safety, and one's refusal to withdraw. Avoiding conflict delays solutions and drives them underground, only to rise again with double fury. Get on with the traditional solution method and see how satisfying it can be.

4) Passive-aggressive conflict managers. These people charge in, then back away and let others manage. They are a mixture of the ostrich and the solution-asserter. Eagerness is cycled with avoidance. The pattern is as follows: hastily attack a problem. But eager haste produces a faulty solution. The faulty solution works terribly, produces guilt, and leads to avoidance. Since guilt needs atonement, another hasty effort is made to make up for the failure. Once again a solution is unlikely and guilt is aroused. Guilt leads to withdrawal. Guilt must be atoned, so another crash solution is tried, and the cycle continues. In time someone else solves the problem so the passive-aggressive person is off the hook. This style of management is usually driven by feelings of inferiority. Since confidence is low, carefully planned solutions are too risky. Haste shortens the time for risk. The result is usually unsatisfactory, unless the solver is awfully lucky.

5) Rational problem solvers study a situation, get important elements identified, and proceed in logical fashion. They see conflict as an opportunity to get useful ideas out and feelings settled. They are comfortable with the traditional method of resolution. They are not plagued by symbolic problems in recycled conflicts. Realism marks progress all along the way. Solutions are varied, and can be modified. Evaluation is not threatening and no one is made to feel blame if all does not go well. Respect for feelings and economical use

of time can be counted upon in discussions. This method can be learned and taught to those with less adaptive techniques.

References

1. Ragan, Pauline, ed. *Aging Parents* (Los Angeles: University of Southern California Press, The Ethel Percy Andrus Gerontology Center, 1979).
2. Ahlem, Lloyd H., *Living With Stress* (Ventura, California: Regal Books, 1978).

Questions for Discussion

1. What kind of conflict participant are you? What do you believe has made you play the role you play in conflict?
2. What have been the gains/losses resulting from conflict in your life over the last several years? Would you have benefited more or less if you had been more or less prone to conflict? Why and how?
3. What kind of issues do you fight about? Have any of these been refocused into symbolic issues and conflicts? What might these be? Should any of them be focused again?
4. How do you deal personally with conflict addicts and people who must have peace at any price?
5. What purpose does conflict serve in your life? Are the purposes essentially productive or unproductive? What evidence gives you your answer?

NINE

Mind, Money, and Emotions

For many years Mrs. J had been the family money manager. Now she lives alone, memory lapses in high gear and picking up speed. Her checkbook is a mess and she can scarcely remember where her assets are. Fortunately she has saved every receipt, check, bill, and bank statement for at least twenty years. Also twenty pounds of rubber bands! All stuffed into one big box except for recent records, which are in her overloaded purse. After a day sorting and arranging, I left her apartment with things in good order, only to return the next morning and find she had pulled out old checks, resorted the records, and worried half the night about not having enough to pay her bills. We reorganized the material and she agreed not to rearrange the piles. I hope she remembers her agreement.

This woman's problem illustrates three points about economics for some retirees. First, they are concerned about having enough money to pay expenses. Second, their emotional relationship to money may foul up important economic decisions. Third, competency may fail when good planning is most crucial. This woman had struggled for years with money and learned to think "poor." Furthermore, she shared her worries with everyone she knew, and they came to believe she was poor. She even convinced her pastor, and was prayed for by her congregation. Her husband died and the time came to sell her house and enter a retirement facility. His costly final illness added to her perception that she was indeed "poor." Several friends approached her retirement center imploring administrators to make special arrangements to alleviate her financial stress. The director of the facility came to me to discuss her situation and see if I could help her get things in order. Then they would reduce fees as necessary.

When I returned to the director, I told him of investments doing well, of a house that had appreciated tremendously, and of an older brother who had left her money as well. Her assets actually exceeded one-half-million dollars. But she was psychologically "poor." When I tried to explain her wealth to her, she was giddy with delight one minute and denying it the next. She found it difficult to part with her poorness because poverty had become a treasured tool to solicit the sympathy of friends. She arrived at the center and immediately tried to bargain about fees. But the administrator talked to her in terms of what she could really afford. She eventually selected a deluxe, two-bedroom, two-bath unit with closed garage. Fine, new furniture was purchased and she settled in. But she still visits the administrator every couple of months seeking a reduction in costs. She has also lost a couple of friends who are no longer convinced she is poor. This woman established her emotional relationship to money years ago when her family was in poverty. She remembers both parents scraping for every penny, suffering through depression while living on an arid farm, unable to finance a high-school education until after she was married. But she and her husband hit upon an economic formula: they would save 10 percent of whatever they earned, no matter how difficult, and they would give 10 percent to church and charity as well. So they went through life with memories of being poor and living with a 20 percent income reduction, even though giving away 10 percent became an especially joyous experience.

Actually this woman was not so different from other young people. Most establish basic attitudes toward money sometime in elementary school years, when they first become aware of it's economic and psychological value. But these feelings are conditioned by parents' attitudes and the economic circumstances of the time. I was a depression kid who picked up dad's pay envelope each month. I would carefully open it, see the amount, and try to reseal it so no one would know I had peeked. That didn't work very well, but dad didn't mind. What a huge sum; $86.33 a month! I figured that to be about $1000 a year. I couldn't imagine what anyone would do with all that cash!

My father was a pastor at the time in a small, struggling church. I learned not to be poverty-minded, but very conservative. To this day, I am not much of a financial risk-taker. My parents were good stewards of their resources and trusted God a lot when the last dollar had to stretch three or four days on our vacations. My first allowance was 10 cents a week and I was expected to tithe a penny to the offering plate on Sunday. I didn't mind, having sensed my parents' attitudes. To this day we practice tithing—and extra giving as well—and have taught our children to do the same. Like Mrs. J, we learned to enjoy it immensely.

Many present retirees were raised in similar circumstances. There are some, however, who resent their economic upbringing and struggle with money many years later when they have much. Their struggles are not economic; they are emotional and spiritual. I have seen joyfully poor people make contributions to the needs of others who have exhausted their resources. Likewise, I have seen well-heeled people groan with pain when any special project is attempted in their churches or communities. Present retirees who grew up in depression days have experienced an economic, emotional yo-yo in their development. They made do with little at first; then following World War II boom times arrived. Homes were built by the millions, highways spanned the nation, cities expanded, two cars appeared in most garages, and higher education became available to nearly anyone academically qualified. People who learned to think "poor" have become better off than they could have imagined. Luxury guilt is common. Emotionally, they never quite got used to affluence.

Economic security has little to do with assets. Poor people can be as miserly as rich people. Rich folks can be generous or niggardly. It all depends upon the spiritual and emotional quality of life. But whatever one's emotional relationship to money, it will be a factor one makes plans for in retirement. You will be making some shifts and these shifts will provoke all the strengths and vulnerabilities within them. None of us should be like the old scrooge who said, "Tis better to give than to receive, but receivin' is good enough for me!" But another generation has come along—baby boomers who arrived in growth times and have a different relationship to money. A throw-away economy was surging when they grew up and the depression of the 1930s was irrelevant history. A brochure from a well-known investment firm recently noted that these boomers are heavily impacting the stock market and will drive stock prices up dramatically in the '90s. With substantial incomes and emotional capacities for risk untempered by depression, they plug cash into investments assuming that the economic rise—to which they are wed from birth—is a normal experience.

What will be their expectations as to retirement? They will impact the retirement scene about 2010, when Social Security funds will be plentiful. But just a couple years later, the drain will be so great that strong measures will be needed to preserve its soundness. We may well have a generation of retirees who are struggling, but who learned to think "rich." The key to happy economic adjustment is to be a steward of assets, not an owner. The earlier in life the emotional shift can be made from owner to steward, the happier a person will be. But it is never too late and a miser can be set free even at 80! All we own in life eventually turns to own us. We choose our masters by what we try to enslave to ourselves; whether it be money, a lusty fantasy life, an emotional addiction to anger, or a love for God's people. The slave you choose rises to become master. How beautiful to be possessed by service, generosity, kindness, and care for others.

Following are five basic elements of good financial planning, especially for seniors. The sooner considered, the better:

1) Living costs will decrease. Costs related to employment—such as suits, uniforms, unreimbursed expenses of entertainment, travel incidentals, and the like—no longer will drain cash. You once paid for services you will now perform yourself: minor plumbing (if you own a wrench and a skilled hand attached to it), lawn services, cleaning, and incidental repairs. You may be pleasantly surprised how much your savings are.

2) Increased health expenditures, with the major portion occurring in final illness. Qualifying for Medicare helps, but Medicare is as good as it is going to get. Only reductions in federal subsidies are in the offing. Many expenses are not covered. Physicians often refuse Medicaid patients—patients who can't pay more than Medicare provides. Nursing home care is very expensive, as are insurance policies to cover it. These expenses have depleted resources for a number of people. It is important to consult carefully with an attorney if this seems likely. Sometimes it is possible to divide assets between husband and wife, thus preventing one spouse from spending the other into poverty. Laws have been changing rapidly in this matter and will change again, I am sure.

Remember that half of the health bill in America is self-inflicted through use of alcohol, tobacco, drugs, and poor diets. You don't really need to smoke, eat sugar, salt, fat, and preservatives at every meal. A healthy lifestyle is one of the best insurance policies available. People with very high incomes pay most for their indulgences and have reduced life expectancy as a result. Disease patterns have changed. With bacterial diseases on the wane, we are left to maladies of the nervous system and viral diseases which are more stubborn than ever. The cost of final illness has inflated more than any other event.

3) Inflation. Recent history shows that living costs have doubled every seven to ten years. At age 65 you are going to have costs double twice by age 85. Ask yourself if you can live on one quarter as much as you now spend. Social Security and some pension programs have cost-of-living increases built in, but these often are not a major portion of one's income. So many retirees slip back in purchasing power a little each year.

Many seniors who begin estate planning have not counted their money very well. Having worked closely with financial planning people through colleges, hospitals, and retirement centers, I know that many older people underestimate their net worth substantially. Occasionally the underestimate is so great the person has not bothered to make a will and leaves substantial sums for heirs to squabble about. So while inflation is nicking away at the value of the dollar, it is also adding value to your assets. In that sense, inflation is not entirely your enemy.

Money is now the most private subject in life, seldom shared openly. Once it was sex, but that has changed. But complete privacy can be a handicap. I know 90 year olds who will not tell their children how much or where their assets are. Withholding such information may appear to be an act of modesty, but the grief it will cause is unnecessary. Less modesty and more trust will solve more problems. A trusted person needs to know—one who can be legally responsible for the good stewardship of your assets.

4) Limiting non-earning assets. It is worth considering switching from assets that you support to assets that support you. Many older people own too much real estate. This depends, of course, on whether the real estate is inflating in value or not, and if the inflation exceeds the cost of maintenance and taxes. Even with substantial increase in value, a lot of the gain is eaten away by insurance, repairs, utilities, taxes, and the work to keep the property in good condition. With a tax break on gains from selling a personal home, trading down or considering a retirement center can save substantial sums.

5) Effective use of estate planning instruments. As you read these sentences remember that this is not legal advice. It is the observation of one who has seen many people move through

financial problems and pleasures, and occasionally a disaster. Whatever you do, get good counsel! Time spent with ethical attorneys and estate planners is an excellent investment! Preparation of three instruments is vital. These are: a well-drawn will, a revocable trust, and a durable power of attorney. Obviously these instruments have rules that vary from state to state. But no one should be uninformed about these three items.

A well-drawn will carries out your wishes and preserves your stewardship of assets through your demise. It prevents more family arguments than it starts. It answers questions others cannot answer after you are gone. It is your most basic document in financial planning. If you don't have one, your state does, and it is thousands of pages long, consisting of more hassle than you ever dreamed possible. But don't let yourself off with a hand-written (holographic) will, either. They are often unclear and easily contested, or invalid. Intelligent people do very stupid things in death they never would have done in life by not having a will. Yet only about one in seven in the United States has one.

The revocable trust is useful in that it provides for the management of your money and gives you income to spend. Someone competent assures that you are well-invested. A second advantage is that assets in a revocable trust need not go through probate. An easy transfer to heirs and beneficiaries is made possible without difficult court proceedings. The trust will have to file an income tax return, but that is a minor inconvenience in view of the benefits. You can also be your own trustee and control the trust as you wish. If it is not useful, you can cancel it.

The third necessary instrument is a durable power of attorney. Again, this instrument will vary in its power and scope from state to state. Most such powers of attorney are divided: power to care for person, and power to care for assets. The same person is often appointed to both functions, but should there be conflict of interest between the two, different individuals should serve. This instrument provides for important health-care and related business decisions to be made according to your wishes when you are unable to decide for yourself. I have never seen a financial tumult when these three instruments are properly drawn and up to date. Again, you are reading a layman's opinion. Get good counsel!

Sometimes in death we can do what we never did in life. I remember a women who spent her life housekeeping for a wealthy southern California family. The family had no spiritual interests, but instead had nearly insatiable appetites for money and pleasure. When they had all passed on, they left a legacy of unhappiness, strife, and bankruptcy. The cleaning woman, who lived very modestly, died without an heir. But a local church received a bequest substantial enough to build a gymnasium that ministered to the needs of hundreds of neighborhood children. She accomplished more in death than her wealthy employers did in all of life.

Or I think of a well-to-do businessman who came to know Christ in his fifties. His conversion was a fountain of joy and he told anyone who would listen about the new life he had received. His pastor challenged him shortly thereafter to give 10 percent of his income to God's work and charity and increase giving by one percent a year afterwards—thus to see if he could outgive God in his blessing. The man died accidentally a few years later, but in his will he had created a substantial trust to continue his giving when he was gone. Most of us will be richest when we are oldest and can enjoy similar opportunities. Don't think small!

Questions for Discussion

1. If you are old enough to remember the great depression, describe your feelings about it. If you are younger, describe how you felt about those who tried to impress you with the magnitude of it. Were they difficult to believe?
2. Describe your earliest memory of money and what it meant to you. Who was influential in shaping your feelings about money when you were very young? What did they say and do?
3. How has your attitude toward money changed over the years? Describe any differences in the way you feel now about it? What anxieties do you have? What is your present definition of economic security?
4. What do the concepts "thinking poor' and "thinking rich" mean to you? How do you think now?
5. What does it mean to have enough money? Have you ever experienced "luxury guilt" or felt you had too much money? Describe these feelings.
6. If you are older, describe how you are handling the competing needs for your own care in advanced years and the need to be generous and a good steward of your resources?
7. How much of your stress in life is economically involved?

8. What emotional effects would you experience if you gained or lost a great deal of money? Describe these.

TEN

Marks of Faith's Maturity

One of my favorite uplifts has been to chat with faith-seasoned older people over coffee. Each one has a story to tell—often fascinating, many times funny. Life's tests have forged character and given them quiet joy. They are peaceful, yet full of reflective humor and wisdom. Multiplied grace makes them gentle, yet sure.

Recently I returned to the university to teach a course in personality theory for a professor on leave, a course I had taught many times and enjoyed a great deal. We worked through the theories, from Sigmund Freud and his various complexes to Abraham Maslow and his traits of self-actualizing people. It's a journey from pessimistic to optimistic psychology, increasingly grabbing students' interests—a delightful way to finish a semester.

Comparing Maslow's self-realized individuals with people I visited over coffee, I found many similar traits: full use of intellectual and emotional powers, freedom from self-doubt and guilt, close ties to a few spiritual peers, a sense of oneness with all humankind; warm, unhostile humor; the capacity to learn from anyone, whether king our scoundrel; and being clear about one's philosophic commitments. To read Maslow[1] was to find words that were attributes of grace I had long taken for granted as normal, maturely developed Christian experience. Yet when Maslow stated his theory and described maturity, he brightened academic psychology with the glow of a fascinating new idea. But I wondered if anyone in psychology ever read about Spirit-filled people as the New Testament describes them. I have known such folks all my life. Is my experience of grace in Christian fellowship so rare that psychologists are just now discovering such traits to be possible? I was startled, for what I took for granted as normal must be unknown to many in academic institutions.

You can get depressed groveling through Freud and the behaviorists. But as self-actualizers are discussed, students react as if they were finding stars by which to navigate through life. Discussions were reflective and lively; feelings of hope turned aside pessimism. Class members began telling their personal stories. One man had lost his homosexual lover and was in grief as a result. A beautiful girl, once a Miss America candidate, told of her demeaning relationship with her father and how she counted on good looks to compensate for inferiorities she had developed. Another, divulging a story of parental molestation, was now living with suppressed rage and wanting badly to retaliate. She also wanted to forgive her parents and herself for allowing herself to be abused, but had no idea how to do it.

Following class I often took my lunch in the cafeteria, wanting to be available to tell my students of the grace that heals—just as I had seen in so many mature older people where I worked. For one student, it was the simple idea that God loves and forgives. For another, it was encouragement that being jilted by a spouse is not fatal either to mind or soul, and grace heals hurts we don't deserve. To yet another, it was the idea that freedom from guilt and debilitation is in God's normal program for everyone. Only recently are psychologists theorizing adequately about that which believers have known for centuries and which aging Christians have tested for decades.

Grace and maturity, multiplied over one's years, is embellished over generations. Christian maturity takes more than one lifetime to produce fully. Individuals seeking instant maturity through a single emotional or spiritual upheaval are kidding themselves. God, in the Old Testament, promised his blessing to faithful men and women and to their children's children. Being a fourth-generation believer—with children who are fifth-generation Christians—I can see the evidences of God's promise in my own family. We need the continuing growth and modeling of faith by older generations to develop and secure the living, growing faith of the young. Sometimes psychological terms give us a fresh look at spiritual and theological subjects. Several years ago David Erb presented a thoughtful address to the Whitworth College dinner at the General Assembly of the Presbyterian Church on the faith development of college students.[2]

I am indebted to him for assisting my thinking in developing the scheme that follows. That development of faith follows identifiable steps:

1) Adoptive faith. We adopt faith from our parents. As such it is reliant on external authority for its ideas—valid because authoritative people in our lives believe it. Parents teach tenets of faith to their children, and children unquestioningly adopt them as their own. Older, new believers adopt the faith of their tutors. Whatever is contained in the parents or tutor's teaching is the sum of personal creed. Words have fixed meanings; concepts are not very flexible.

One evening when my son was about ten years old, he answered the door to find a pollster who wanted to know the political affiliation of our home. "What are we, Dad?" he shouted across the living room, "Democrats or Republicans?" "Republicans!" I retorted, "Like good Christians should be!" He turned to relay the reply to the pollster when he suddenly realized he had been duped and made to feel foolish. The pollster got a good laugh and went on his way. But the timing was right for a discovery by my son. Bright enough to think a few things out for himself, he saw the folly of linking "Republican" and "Christian" together. From that time on he was more questioning about what we told him and evaluated ideas more carefully. By the time he was a high school junior he had written a paper on C.S. Lewis's theology of heaven and hell for a totally secular English teacher who rewarded him with an "A." Watching him mature into a thoughtful, Christian adult has been a great pleasure.

Unfortunately, some never get past adoptive belief. Simple formulations become the whole of the matter and they never wrestle with the problems or concepts to make them their own. Perhaps they have assumed that any difference from parents' ideas was heresy and feared critical thinking was devilish behavior. Unfortunately, untested belief doesn't stand tough questioning or tough times, and faith as well as growth can be squelched.

2) Reactive faith. The content of reactive faith is the same as in adoptive faith, but the believer handles ideas oppositionally. He or she introduces no new concepts, but acts simply to test the authority of the one who taught. This person is like the adolescent who regards adult authority as something to mistrust. In resisting he or she doesn't provide anything to replace adults' ideas, but by negative stance separates emotionally from parents, establishing independence. Some young people get stuck at this stage, remaining in faith but

negative about it. Basic concepts aren't regarded as satisfactory, but new ground is unbroken.

I once met a Bible teacher in a Christian college, still reactive though very well-educated. His parents were devoutly simplistic and denied any need to work through beliefs delivered by their predecessors. So the professor, irritated by parents' restrictive thinking, found a haven in his professorship to teach reactive faith to his classes. Trying to solve his own problem he created more of them by tearing down simple concepts held by students. But unable to lead them to anything more, he was constantly in hot water with parents who had sent their children to a Christian school to keep them in adoptive faith.

Apparently most youngsters can achieve about one stage beyond their parents in faith development. But two or more steps is too uncomfortable. If parents hold a simplistic, adoptive faith themselves, the most the children will achieve is a reactive faith. Adults who get stuck in reactive faith often remain believers but become critics of both faith and church without ever denying any of faith's tenets. Unfortunately, when they teach their children, they begin oppositionally and are likely to produce a high drop-out rate from church and parents' commitments. Or the parents revert to an adoptive level to save their children from sacking their beliefs. But to stay in reactive faith is not very healthy emotionally and precarious spiritually. It is like spending a lifetime as an adolescent; never a child and never mature.

3) Self-confirmed faith. At this level, believers have turned from negative to positive ideas and language. Adolescent challenges to parents concepts are over; authority figures are helpful, not antagonists. Faith feels good and believers are satisfied with their growth. But self-confirmed commitments do not maintain relationships with other believers. Too often they have found simpler believers more problem than reinforcement and stand aloof from the church. Satisfied with their faith and feeling as if they have come to it on their own, they are not likely to become productive members of the faith community. At least not until they discover that ultimately we all live by the grace of God even if we have become smart enough to go it alone for awhile.

4) Integrated faith. At this level it is possible to make important faith commitments without all the theological wrinkles worked out. The negations of level 2 are inverted so that differences of experience

help to increase understanding and are highly valued for stimulating mature inquiry. Differences become treasured rather than feared and are no longer in contest with other faith experiences.

In one denominational college it was found that a few students reached self-confirmed faith and no students reached integrated faith. As a result, strategy for spiritual formation and instruction in religion was altered. If students have to grow past parents to become mature, rather than grow up to them, they would need a great deal of help with the troubled feelings that might result. Furthermore, if it is true that faith is the product of more than one generation of Christian experience, students should have the best beginning and most mature perspective possible. If they could possibly be brought to integrated faith, they would be leading the previous generation, not following it and stumbling when its growth ceased. So a new, ambitious goal was adopted by the faculty.

Deep fellowship is the great fulfillment of integrated faith. Hangups are past, each believer cherishes the experience of the other, and mutual support is given and received without being stuck together in codependent binds. Ministry can be offered without creating debts for recipients. The church can become productive without struggling through endless personal and doctrinal squabbles. People have been set free, even as Scripture asserts: "For freedom Christ has set you free" (Galatians 5:1). Egos take second place to the spiritual well-being of the community.

The number of believers that mature to this fourth level is likely to be small. With a mobile society breaking up fellowship groups, with people dropping out of immature faith in substantial numbers, with many believers entrenched in adoptive faith, it may be difficult to achieve full development of faith in large numbers. I also think the television church highlights dependency in adoptive faith, infusing it with a great deal of emotional value. Messages are seldom developed that require great insight and depth of understanding. Unless a person has grown in a church that has known maturity in its membership for more than a generation, the opportunities for full faith development may be limited.

Therefore, what is needed and possible is continued growth through our later years. Instant maturity is clearly a myth and we need to plan for progress over a long period of time. If older members will forge ahead, finding full faith development, their lives will create an environment for a following generation to break its limits. They will grow spiritually without stress by moving more than one stage ahead of their parents. Aging is not an excuse for stalled maturity. Older people mark the limits of faith development for younger generations. If the boundaries are limited the whole body is restricted in growth. Younger believers need to grow up to the most mature in the congregation, not past them with turmoil in the process.

Another major idea important to faith development is that mature spiritual experience involves a radically different personality organization. It is different because every theory of personality assumes that ego is the central point and purpose of self-development. From Freud to Maslow, through 75 years of theory building, this assumption has been held. Unfortunately, every theory is empirically correct while theologically wrong. Correct because self-seeking is the inevitable striving of every individual. Every person seeks to play god in life or to follow a god of his or her own making. Wrong, because self-seeking inevitably leads to selfishness, frustration, and loss of values that transcend our narrow-minded concerns. The 1980s are looked upon as the decade of the self-seeker. Casualty rates were high as indulgence led to economic and personal crises. One noted journalist and psychologist, Daniel Yankelovich, has written, "The old injunction that to find oneself one must lose himself is a truth any self-seeker needs to grasp."

An important mark of maturity is the degree to which self has been set aside and God placed in the center of life. Setting aside self is an act of surrender that is resisted furiously in most of us. Engrossed in selfish interests we can see only losses when faced with the need to end self-rule. We are most reluctant converts to someone else's lordship, at least until chaos and confusion have nearly destroyed our best-laid plans. But the paradox of finding oneself by losing oneself has taxed the imaginations of saints and sinners for eons. It was faced by a wealthy young ruler who came to Jesus, only to recognize that his possessions were his god, and to turn again to himself. It was also faced by a wealthy young Italian who denied himself no gratification he could imagine. But he turned not to himself but to the lordship of Christ. That man was St. Augustine.

Spiritual maturity, the ultimate purpose of aging, is marked by paradox. If I surrender my career to the direction of God, I have also surrendered the stress of clawing and climbing for prestige. If I surrender my pride in myself I have also lost most of my need to defend myself in any circumstance. If I give up my desires to accumulate wealth, I also lose my inclination to be narrowly focused on economic security, and can be captured by the joys of generosity. When I cease struggling for status, position, or recognition, I lose my defensiveness and become open to people who are put off by such baggage. When I dump my pride in my morality and character, I cease fighting for my most treasured self-image. If I free myself from my need to control, I am suddenly a lover. But only in each case if these cessations are done in the Spirit of Christ.

Our egos were designed to be orbital, not nuclear in our personality organization. Every theory has it the other way around. Our self-fulfillment was planned by God to be a by-product of spiritual development, not an achievement for its own sake. Self-actualization achieved as a secondary effect exceeds the fulfillment sought as an end in itself. The Apostle Paul had it straight: "From now on, therefore, we regard no one from a human point of view. . . . Therefore, if any one is in Christ, he is a new creation, the old has passed away, behold the new has come" (2 Corinthians 5:16-17). We have been given a lifetime to become new people. In advanced years, we lose most of the capacities to be anything but new people, unless we choose to be barren, spiritual curmudgeons. If age strips us of power to pursue false gods, our losses are gifts from the Divine.

References
1. Maslow, Abraham H., *Perceiving, Behaving, Becoming* (Washington, D.C., Asco Yearbook, 1962).
2. Erb, David L., "Faith Development and the Implications for the Church" (unpublished and undated).

Questions for Discussion

1. Interview a person over 75 years of age in regard to his or her faith development? What was their first awareness of spiritual need? What did they do about that awareness and need? What conclusions have they come to in understanding their relationship to God? What does Christ mean to them today? What level of faith development have they reached?
2. Using Weyerhauser's concepts, what level of faith development best describes your present experience? How well does the concept fit your experience?
3. Weyehauser suggests that if we are more than one stage removed from our parents, relationships in faith matters may be difficult to discuss? Have you found this true? Would you agree

with Weyerhauser?
4. In what ways has your faith benefited from the development of previous generations. Has it been impaired or made difficult because of the experience of previous generations? At what stage do you find yourself today?
5. What is your emotional response to your faith? Is it satisfying? Anxiety producing? A hindrance or help to your intellectual understanding of faith?
6. What is your spiritual goal in life? How would you like to live your spiritual life? What guides you to that goal?
7. What kind of people do you have difficulty with in sharing your faith? What accounts for this difficulty?
8. What has been your most important experience in your Christian life of faith as you have matured?

ELEVEN

Considering a Care or Retirement Center

If you are considering a retirement center for yourself or making arrangements for a parent, a number of questions must be asked before you make your move. This is a major adjustment in life, and if badly planned can result in much unhappiness. On the other hand, many have been delightfully pleased. A common expression I hear is, "I should have done this a couple of years earlier. I was ready two years before I realized it."

Use the following questions as a test to determine your readiness for the move you are considering:

1) How do I feel about making this move? Happy? Guilty? Ambivalent? Why? Mixed emotions are very common. A fine facility can be an inviting place. Some are so fashionable and deluxe they prompt gasps when first seen. Not a few people feel luxury guilt about entering sparkling new residences. But they are available, attractive, and costs need not be prohibitive. Such a move is likely your last one. Recognize the finality of it. It is important.

Moving means scaling down the size of living quarters. Most have lived in three- and four-bedroom homes and move to one- or two-bedroom apartments. This adjustment takes a few months, some of it before the move is made. Disposal of unneeded household items isn't always easy; emotional attachments have been made to special pieces. But this is part of the transition, not part of the eventual solution. I know no one who has suffered very long by scaling down. Usually it results in convenience and unburdening. Most of us have accumulated more than we can use.

Try to interview yourself. Ask tough questions about your "gut" reactions. Feelings are often masked and need to be uncovered. If resentment is harbored, that feeling will be dumped on other residents and staff. Some would be better off emotionally to stick it out in their own homes if bad feelings abound. Some do not come to terms easily with their limited remaining years and capacities and might be better off with other arrangements. Unfortunately, such people are headed for more difficulty, no matter what arrangement they make.

Sometimes a move cannot be prevented, as happens when care in a nursing facility is needed immediately. In such cases, the emotional adjustment is made after the fact. That probably doesn't shorten the adjustment period; it just changes its location. People need help getting used to new circumstances and it is always counter-productive to hurry them into acceptance. The shock of moving will last a couple of weeks. Then several months may be needed to go through the cycle of descending morale, with its feelings of depression. But the human mind is wonderfully made—and with encouragement hope rises again and the future will look attractive.

2) Can I reach an understanding with the people who are close to me? For adult children assisting their parents, understanding is critical. Allow plenty of wiggle room so feelings can be expressed. Fast moves are usually bad moves. Most residents have been on a waiting list for admission and have had advance time to absorb the full meaning of their moves. But we have seen sons or daughters come from distant places and, without much notice, wrench parents out of familiar surroundings and dump them in a retirement center. They were bothered that the parents did not appreciate the idea and wept most of the weekend. When the move was completed the children returned to their homes not recognizing the havoc they had caused. A necessary move eventually became a happy one, but the parents were angry a long time over the way the move was managed.

3) Can I trust the care given or must I become highly concerned? Talk to others in the facility you are considering. Are they spontaneously happy when they speak about it? Do you hear about problems continuously? What do you see and feel when you visit? Much bad publicity has been given to care facilities that do not serve well. But the great majority deserve appreciation. Visit long enough to sense the morale of residents and patients. This may be your most important clue to the quality of the facility. Be assured before you move.

4) What is the mission and purpose of the facility you are

considering? Is it a ministry of a well-established church or benevolent organization? Is it simply a venture to profit from increasing numbers of seniors who are living longer with plenty of assets to spend? I know one chain of care centers that budgets its profit-margin first, then squeezes all other expenses to assure that the profit is made. On the other hand, I do know facilities—usually church-related—that regard their work as ministry; their first concern is care for people. In broad theological terms, it is the purpose of the church to preach, to teach, and to heal. Christian care centers and retirement homes are integral parts of the last of these three purposes. As years pass the motives within the mission will become very apparent and will dominate the quality of the service given.

5) What is the attitude of personnel? Talk to housekeepers, waitresses, and office staff. Are they defensive? Do they enjoy serving? Are they only stopping by on their way to better-paying jobs? Do they have punitive motives? In a study of quality of life in the centers I worked for it was discovered that service personnel got higher ratings from residents than administrative people. That was good news, for it meant that people closest to residents were highly regarded. Administrative people are a little more distant, dealing with larger-scale matters. Do the staff seem to be controlling or dominating in their attitudes? If this attitude is present, independence and freedom will be limited—a condition not conducive to happiness or good health.

6) What kind of people live in the center? Poor? Rich? Infirm? Odd? From one particular sect or group? We are most comfortable with people whose demeanor and values are similar to our own. I know a retirement home that is new, beautiful, and well-managed. But its architecture, style, staff, and residents represent one small ethnic group. The home is open to all who might afford its services but the administrator can't understand why more people don't rush to live there. Residents don't want to feel like guests, forever at someone else's family reunion. If you feel strangely about the mood or climate of a facility, ask questions about its background and lifestyle. When we feel right about a place we can depend on the facility being supportive of us, especially when difficulties arise. Then we'll be handled in ways that we accept and find helpful.

7) What specific health care is provided? Bedside nursing? Care in an assisted-living facility? Skilled nursing? Hospitalization? Psychiatric care? Physical therapy? Transportation to medical facilities? Special

facilities for Alzheimer's or Parkinson's disease? These are contractual details that need spelling out. Be sure to read a copy of the residency agreement or contract before making a decision. Keep the copy and mark it up with your questions. Understand fully what insurance you are expected to provide and what the facility provides. What happens when you can no longer afford the costs? Will you be asked to leave? Or is this a life-care facility that sees you through to the end of life? The most difficult problem is to be turned away when you need assistance most. If you sense in any way that your questions are being avoided or not answered fully, find out why. Every credible, ethical facility is eager to help you know the answers.

8) How well is the center maintained? Is it clean? Shabby? Smelly? Is the furniture in good repair? Maintenance is a clue to the self-image of a facility. If a center has high regard for itself, it will have a fine appearance. I do not know a facility that looks tacky or unkempt that gives good service over time. Ask about maintenance policies and capital budgets. These are indications of the attitude of the center toward itself and you.

9) How is the center financed? Do you pay an entry fee and what does it cover? What are the monthly fees and how are they calculated? Is the center in sound financial condition? Will they give you a financial statement? Is the latest audit report available? How much of your payment goes to debt service? Does the state require reserves to care for you if financial difficulty overtakes the institution? Can you get your money back if you change your mind shortly after entering? How much will you get? If you leave in a year or two will you also get something back? How is the refund calculated? As you can see, a lot of questions can be asked and if answers are not forthcoming, don't sign in.

Most centers are highly regulated by state and federal government. These centers must know their costs, the life-expectancy of residents, and the laws concerning management. They are accountable to regulators and inspectors. It is also useful to contact state regulatory agencies for reports of inspections. These are public records and can be seen by prospects. There is no need to be fooled or surprised by economic or management problems.

10) What is the history and reputation of the center? Who makes its public statements? Who guarantees its future financial as well as spiritual viability? How long has it been in business? How has it built its reputation? What does the community say about the facility? The

organization I work for has been operating for more than 100 years. There are others of long-standing Christian reputation and service. In my view, the best ones have a clear Christian mission, will be tax-exempt, non-profit facilities, will be completely open to you for examination and inquiry, and present themselves as clean, well-maintained, modern facilities with service-minded staff. They will have adequate documentation of all their contracts, their financial condition, and regulatory reviews—and you can see all of these.

NOTES

NOTES

NOTES

NOTES